All About San Diego: A Kid's Guide to America's Finest City

Educational Books For Kids, Volume 49

Anam Rasheed

Published by Anam Rasheed, 2025.

While every precaution has been taken in the preparation of this book, the publisher assumes no responsibility for errors or omissions, or for damages resulting from the use of the information contained herein.

ALL ABOUT SAN DIEGO: A KID'S GUIDE TO AMERICA'S FINEST CITY

First edition. March 4, 2025.

Copyright © 2025 Anam Rasheed.

ISBN: 979-8230699934

Written by Anam Rasheed.

Table of Contents

Prologue......1
Chapter 1: Sunny Beaches and Ocean Waves......2
Chapter 2: The Amazing San Diego Zoo......6
Chapter 3: Exploring Balboa Park......10
Chapter 4: History at Old Town......14
Chapter 5: The Wonders of SeaWorld......18
Chapter 6: A Day at Mission Bay......22
Chapter 7: Wildlife at Safari Park......26
Chapter 8: Adventures on Coronado Island......30
Chapter 9: Discovering Little Italy......34
Chapter 10: Fun at LEGOLAND......38
Chapter 11: Ships and Stories at Maritime Museum......42
Chapter 12: Hiking in Torrey Pines......46
Chapter 13: Science Fun at Fleet Center......49
Chapter 14: Shopping in Seaport Village......53
Chapter 15: Delicious Mexican Food......57
Chapter 16: Sports and Stadiums......61
Chapter 17: Festivals and Parades......65
Chapter 18: Ghost Stories of Old San Diego......69
Chapter 19: Music and Art Scenes......73
Chapter 20: Sunset Views from La Jolla......77
Epilogue......81

Prologue

Welcome to San Diego, the city of endless sunshine, sandy beaches, and exciting adventures! Known as "America's Finest City," San Diego is a place where fun and history come together like no other. Here, you can visit world-famous attractions, explore beautiful parks, and even learn about fascinating cultures from around the globe.

Have you ever wondered what it's like to see a giant panda at the San Diego Zoo, or to watch dolphins leap high above the waves at SeaWorld? What about walking through the historic streets of Old Town, where California began? Or maybe you'd love to splash around Mission Bay or go on an adventure at LEGOLAND? In San Diego, all these adventures are waiting for you!

But there's more to this city than just fun and games. San Diego is bursting with stories from the past, incredible wildlife, delicious food, and vibrant neighborhoods that each have their own unique charm. From the thrilling tales of explorers and sailors to the colorful festivals that light up the streets, there's always something new to discover.

So, grab your explorer's hat and get ready to dive into the magic of San Diego. This book is your guide to the best spots, coolest activities, and most exciting secrets of this amazing city. Whether you're planning a visit or just curious about this sunny corner of California, you're in for a fantastic journey.

Are you ready to explore America's Finest City? Let's go!

Chapter 1: Sunny Beaches and Ocean Waves

San Diego is famous for its warm, sunny weather and breathtaking beaches that stretch along the Pacific Ocean. The golden sands and rolling waves make it a paradise for anyone who loves the outdoors. Whether you want to splash in the water, build a sandcastle, or just relax under the bright blue sky, the beaches of San Diego have something for everyone. The ocean breeze carries the salty scent of the sea, and the sound of waves crashing against the shore is like nature's own music. With miles and miles of coastline, there are plenty of different beaches to explore, each with its own special charm and exciting activities.

Some beaches in San Diego are perfect for swimming because the waves are gentle, and the water is calm. These beaches have lifeguards watching over swimmers to make sure everyone stays safe. The soft sand feels warm underfoot, and you might even spot tiny seashells or pieces of colorful sea glass washed up by the tide. Other beaches are great for surfing, with big, rolling waves that challenge surfers to ride them all the way to the shore. People come from all over the world to surf in San Diego because the waves are just right, and the weather is almost always perfect for catching a wave. Beginners can take surfing lessons, while experienced surfers show off their skills, balancing on their boards as they glide across the water.

One of the best things about San Diego's beaches is that they are home to many different kinds of animals. If you take a walk along the shore, you might see tiny crabs scurrying across the sand or seabirds diving into the water to catch fish. In the tide pools, which are small pools of seawater left behind when the tide goes out, you can discover sea stars, sea anemones, and little fish hiding in the rocks. If you're lucky, you might even spot dolphins swimming just beyond the waves or see a sea lion basking in the sun on a rocky shoreline. During certain times of the year, you can watch gray whales as they migrate along the coast, moving between the cold waters of Alaska and the warm waters of Mexico.

Some of the most famous beaches in San Diego include La Jolla Shores, Mission Beach, Pacific Beach, and Coronado Beach. La Jolla Shores is a great place for families because the water is calm, and there's plenty of space to play. It's also a great spot for kayaking and snorkeling, where you can see colorful fish and even leopard sharks, which are harmless to humans. Mission Beach is known for its lively boardwalk, where people ride bikes, rollerblade, and stop at little shops to get ice cream or snacks. Pacific Beach is a popular spot for young people and surfers, with lots of restaurants and surf shops nearby. Coronado Beach, with its sparkling sand made of tiny pieces of crushed shells, is famous for its stunning views and the historic Hotel del Coronado, which looks like a castle by the sea.

Beach days in San Diego aren't just about swimming and surfing. There are so many fun things to do along the shore! Some people love playing beach volleyball, digging their feet into the sand as they jump and dive to hit the ball. Others enjoy flying kites, watching as the wind lifts them high into the sky, their bright colors standing out against the deep blue ocean. Families bring picnic baskets filled with delicious food, spreading out blankets to enjoy lunch with the sound of the waves in the background. Kids love collecting seashells, searching for the prettiest or most unusual ones to take home as souvenirs. And when the sun starts to set, bonfires light up the beaches, with people gathering around to roast marshmallows and tell stories.

The ocean waves in San Diego are always moving, bringing new adventures with every tide. At high tide, the waves come up farther onto the shore, making it exciting to jump over them or let them wash over your feet. At low tide, the water pulls back, revealing hidden treasures like smooth pebbles, tiny sand dollars, and even bits of driftwood that have traveled far across the sea. The waves are created by the wind and the pull of the moon, and they come in all different shapes and sizes. Some are small and gentle, perfect for wading and splashing, while others are tall and powerful, thrilling surfers as they rush toward the shore.

The weather in San Diego makes its beaches even more special. With more than 260 sunny days a year, there are very few times when it's too cold to visit the beach. Even in winter, people still enjoy walking along the shore, watching the waves, and breathing in the fresh ocean air. The sun shines down, making the water sparkle like a million tiny diamonds, and the cool breeze keeps it from feeling too hot. Sometimes, in the early morning, a light mist rolls in from the ocean, making the beach look mysterious and magical. But by midday, the sun usually burns away the mist, revealing a clear, bright sky.

San Diego's beaches are not just for fun—they are also important for nature and the environment. The dunes, cliffs, and wetlands near the shore provide homes for many kinds of animals, including rare birds and sea creatures. People work hard to keep the beaches clean by picking up trash and making sure not to disturb the wildlife. Many visitors take part in beach cleanups, helping to protect the beautiful coastline so that future generations can enjoy it too. There are also marine conservation programs that teach people about the ocean and the creatures that live in it, helping everyone understand why it's so important to take care of the sea.

Visiting the beach in San Diego is a magical experience, whether you're dipping your toes in the water, watching the sunset, or listening to the soothing sound of the waves. Every beach has its own special personality, from the peaceful coves of La Jolla to the energetic shores of Mission Beach. No matter where you go, the ocean welcomes you with open arms, inviting you to play, explore, and enjoy the beauty of nature. Whether it's your first visit or your hundredth, San Diego's sunny beaches and ocean waves always have something new and exciting to offer!

Chapter 2: The Amazing San Diego Zoo

The San Diego Zoo is one of the most famous zoos in the world, and for good reason! Located in Balboa Park, this incredible place is home to thousands of animals from all over the planet. With more than 100 acres of land filled with lush greenery, winding pathways, and carefully designed habitats, the zoo is like stepping into a wild adventure. It's not just a place to see animals—it's a place where visitors can learn about wildlife, explore different ecosystems, and discover how scientists and zookeepers work to protect endangered species. The San Diego Zoo is more than 100 years old and has grown into a world leader in animal care, conservation, and education.

One of the most amazing things about the zoo is how natural the animal habitats look. Instead of keeping animals in small cages, the San Diego Zoo creates large, open spaces that look just like the animals' homes in the wild. For example, the African Plains exhibit looks like the grasslands of Africa, where giraffes, rhinos, and gazelles roam freely. The Lost Forest is filled with trees, vines, and waterfalls, making it the perfect home for monkeys, orangutans, and tropical birds. The Arctic area is designed to be cold and icy, just right for polar bears. Each part of the zoo transports visitors to a different part of the world, from the rainforests of Asia to the deserts of North America.

One of the biggest highlights of the zoo is its collection of giant pandas. For many years, the San Diego Zoo was one of the few places outside of China where people could see these rare black-and-white bears. The zoo worked closely with Chinese scientists to study pandas and help increase their population. Although the pandas returned to China in 2019, their legacy at the zoo remains strong, and the conservation work they inspired continues. Visitors can still learn all about pandas and see other amazing animals from China, such as red pandas and golden monkeys.

Another incredible area is the Elephant Odyssey. Here, visitors can see majestic elephants up close and learn about their history, behavior, and the efforts to protect them in the wild. The exhibit is designed to resemble California thousands of years ago when ancient relatives of elephants, like mammoths and mastodons, roamed the land. Alongside the elephants, you can find fossils, statues, and even living descendants of prehistoric animals, like the California condor. It's like traveling back in time while standing right in the middle of a modern zoo.

The San Diego Zoo is also famous for its big cats. The Tiger Trail takes visitors deep into a tropical jungle where they can watch powerful tigers move through their lush habitat. The lions have a huge, open area that looks like the African savanna, and they love to stretch out in the sun or play with each other. There are also speedy cheetahs, mysterious leopards, and even snow leopards that are perfectly adapted to life in cold, mountainous regions. Seeing these incredible predators up close is a breathtaking experience.

For those who love birds, the San Diego Zoo is a paradise. With more than 300 different species of birds, from tiny hummingbirds to giant Andean condors, the zoo is filled with colorful feathers and beautiful songs. One of the most impressive areas is the Owens Aviary, a huge, open-air enclosure where visitors can walk among tropical birds flying freely. Brightly colored parrots, graceful flamingos, and rare hornbills can be seen flapping their wings and calling to each other. Some birds are so friendly that they might even come close to say hello!

If reptiles and amphibians are your thing, the San Diego Zoo has plenty of those too. The Reptile House is home to giant snakes, mysterious lizards, and fascinating frogs from around the world. You can see crocodiles lounging in the water, giant tortoises slowly moving across their habitat, and even venomous vipers coiled up in their enclosures. The Komodo dragon, the world's largest lizard, is one of the most popular residents. It looks like a creature from prehistoric times, with its rough skin, long tail, and sharp claws.

One of the most exciting parts of visiting the zoo is getting to see animals in action. Every day, there are special shows and presentations where zookeepers introduce animals to the audience and explain fun facts about them. Some shows feature birds swooping through the air, while others let visitors see up-close encounters with animals like armadillos, porcupines, and sloths. These shows are a great way to learn about how animals live, what they eat, and how humans can help protect them.

For kids and families, there are plenty of hands-on activities throughout the zoo. The Children's Zoo is a special area where young visitors can pet friendly animals, learn about animal care, and even try out fun science experiments. There's also the Skyfari, a gondola ride that takes visitors high above the zoo, giving them a bird's-eye view of the entire park. From up in the air, you can see elephants walking, monkeys swinging through trees, and flamingos standing in their ponds. It's a great way to take a break from walking while still enjoying the beauty of the zoo.

The San Diego Zoo is also a leader in conservation, which means it works hard to protect animals and their habitats around the world. Scientists at the zoo study endangered animals and find ways to help them survive in the wild. They have special breeding programs for species that are at risk of disappearing, such as the California condor and the black rhino. The zoo also supports conservation projects in other countries, helping to protect rainforests, grasslands, and oceans where animals live. Visitors to the zoo learn about these efforts and discover ways they can help, like recycling, saving water, and supporting wildlife charities.

No visit to the zoo would be complete without exploring some of the more unique and unusual animals. The nocturnal house is home to creatures that are most active at night, like owls, bats, and aardvarks. The hippos love to swim in their big pool, sometimes playfully opening their huge mouths. There are even adorable koalas, which spend most of their time sleeping in eucalyptus trees. The variety of animals at the San Diego Zoo is endless, and every visit brings new surprises.

Because the zoo is so big, it can take an entire day to see everything, but there are plenty of places to rest and grab a snack along the way. There are restaurants and food stands serving everything from sandwiches to ice cream, and plenty of shaded picnic areas where families can relax. Gift shops sell stuffed animals, books, and fun souvenirs so visitors can take a piece of their zoo adventure home with them.

The San Diego Zoo isn't just a place to see animals—it's a place to experience the wonders of the natural world. Whether you're watching a tiger prowl through the jungle, seeing a giraffe stretch its long neck to reach leaves, or laughing at a playful monkey swinging from a tree, every moment is full of excitement and discovery. It's no wonder that millions of people visit the San Diego Zoo every year. It's a magical place where people of all ages can connect with animals, learn about nature, and be inspired to help protect the planet. Every visit is a new adventure, filled with unforgettable sights, sounds, and experiences!

Chapter 3: Exploring Balboa Park

Balboa Park is one of the most exciting and beautiful places in San Diego, filled with gardens, museums, theaters, and so many things to explore that you could spend days here and still not see everything. It's not just any park—it's a cultural wonderland where history, nature, art, and science come together in one magical place. Covering 1,200 acres, it's even bigger than New York's Central Park! People from all over the world visit Balboa Park to stroll through its gorgeous landscapes, admire its stunning Spanish-style buildings, and discover the countless attractions hidden within its borders. Whether you love animals, art, history, or just being outdoors, there's something for everyone in this amazing park.

The story of Balboa Park begins in the 1860s when the city of San Diego set aside a huge area of land to create a public park. At first, it was just open space with trees and hills, but over time, it became something truly special. In 1915, the park was transformed for the Panama-California Exposition, a grand event celebrating the opening of the Panama Canal. Beautiful Spanish-style buildings, elegant fountains, and lush gardens were built for the event, and many of them still stand today. Walking through the park feels like stepping into another world, where the past and present blend together in a spectacular way.

One of the most popular attractions in Balboa Park is the San Diego Zoo. Located right inside the park, the zoo is home to thousands of animals from all over the world, including elephants, lions, tigers, and monkeys. It's one of the most famous zoos in the world, attracting millions of visitors every year. But the zoo is just one of the many amazing things to see in Balboa Park. There are more than 17 museums covering everything from history to space to art, each one packed with exciting exhibits waiting to be explored.

For those who love science, the Fleet Science Center is a must-visit. It's filled with hands-on exhibits where visitors can experiment with physics, engineering, and space exploration. There's even a giant IMAX theater that shows breathtaking documentaries about nature, the universe, and history. Kids and adults alike love the interactive displays, where they can learn about electricity, robotics, and even how astronauts live in space.

Art lovers will be amazed by the San Diego Museum of Art, which houses incredible paintings and sculptures from around the world. The museum's collection includes works by famous artists from Europe, Asia, and the Americas. Walking through its grand galleries, visitors can see masterpieces that are hundreds of years old, as well as modern works by contemporary artists. Just outside the museum, the Plaza de Panama is a beautiful open square where people gather to listen to music, watch performances, or simply enjoy the scenery.

One of the most unique museums in Balboa Park is the Museum of Man. Located inside a stunning Spanish-style building with a tall tower, this museum is all about the history of people and cultures from around the world. Visitors can learn about ancient Egypt, the Maya civilization, and even the science of human evolution. The museum also has an exhibit on monsters and myths from different cultures, showing how legends of dragons, mermaids, and giants have fascinated people for centuries.

If you're fascinated by planes and space travel, the San Diego Air & Space Museum is the place to go. Inside, visitors can see real aircraft, from old-fashioned biplanes to modern fighter jets. There are even replicas of famous spacecraft, like the Apollo command module that took astronauts to the moon! The museum tells the story of aviation history, from the earliest flying machines to the future of space exploration.

For those who love history, the San Diego Natural History Museum is packed with fascinating exhibits about dinosaurs, ancient fossils, and the wildlife of California. Gigantic dinosaur skeletons tower over visitors, while displays of gemstones, insects, and ocean creatures reveal the wonders of the natural world. The museum also has special exhibits about earthquakes, volcanoes, and the forces that have shaped the Earth over millions of years.

One of the most magical places in Balboa Park is the Botanical Building, a breathtaking structure made of wood and glass, filled with exotic plants and flowers from around the world. Stepping inside feels like entering a tropical jungle, where towering ferns, colorful orchids, and trickling fountains create a peaceful oasis. Right outside the building is the Lily Pond, a beautiful pool of water surrounded by gardens. Visitors love to sit by the pond, watching the reflections of the trees and the occasional ducks gliding across the water.

Balboa Park is also home to the Old Globe Theatre, one of the most famous theaters in the United States. Modeled after Shakespeare's Globe Theatre in London, this beautiful building hosts plays and performances all year round. Watching a play here is an unforgettable experience, as the actors bring stories to life on stage in a setting that feels like stepping back in time. The theater hosts a mix of classic plays, modern performances, and even fun productions for kids.

For visitors who love trains, the San Diego Model Railroad Museum is a hidden treasure. This massive museum features miniature train displays that show landscapes, mountains, and tiny cities in amazing detail. The trains move along their tracks, crossing tiny bridges and passing through tunnels. It's the largest model railroad museum in the world, and people of all ages are fascinated by the intricate details and craftsmanship of the displays.

One of the best things about Balboa Park is its outdoor spaces. There are gardens, walking trails, and peaceful picnic spots everywhere. The Japanese Friendship Garden is a serene place with beautiful koi ponds, elegant bridges, and carefully arranged plants that create a sense of peace and harmony. The Desert Garden showcases cacti and succulents from around the world, proving that even in dry environments, plants can be incredibly beautiful. The Alcazar Garden is inspired by the gardens of Spain, with colorful tile fountains and neatly trimmed hedges.

Throughout the year, Balboa Park hosts all kinds of exciting events and festivals. The December Nights festival is one of the biggest celebrations, where the park is decorated with twinkling lights, and visitors can enjoy music, dance, and delicious food from around the world. There are also outdoor concerts, art fairs, and cultural performances that bring the park to life with energy and creativity.

Exploring Balboa Park is like taking a journey through time, nature, and culture all in one place. Whether you're admiring the beautiful architecture, learning about history in a museum, or simply enjoying a picnic under the shade of a tree, there's something new to discover around every corner. It's a place where families can spend a whole day together, where students can learn in a fun and exciting way, and where nature and art exist side by side in perfect harmony. No matter how many times you visit, there's always something new to see, making Balboa Park one of the most unforgettable places in San Diego!

Chapter 4: History at Old Town

Old Town San Diego is like stepping into a time machine and traveling back to the early days of California. It is a place filled with history, culture, and stories of the people who helped shape the city of San Diego. This special part of the city is known as the "Birthplace of California" because it was here that Spanish settlers built the first permanent European settlement in the state. Walking through Old Town feels like entering a different era, where old adobe buildings, dusty streets, and historic sites tell the story of how San Diego grew from a small village into the bustling city it is today.

Long before Spanish explorers arrived, this land was home to the Kumeyaay people, Native Americans who had lived in the region for thousands of years. They built homes, hunted animals, and gathered food from the land. They were experts in using natural resources to create tools, baskets, and pottery. The Kumeyaay had a deep connection to nature, believing that the land, water, and animals were sacred. Even today, their influence can be seen in Old Town, where museums and cultural centers celebrate their traditions and contributions.

In 1769, Spanish explorers led by Gaspar de Portolá and Father Junípero Serra arrived in the area, bringing their customs, religion, and way of life. They built the first mission in California, Mission San Diego de Alcalá, which became an important center for spreading Christianity and European culture. The Spanish also built a military fort, called the Presidio, on a hill overlooking Old Town. This fort protected the settlers from potential attacks and helped establish control over the region. Over time, more Spanish families arrived, and small adobe homes, shops, and farms were built, forming the beginnings of a town.

For many years, Old Town remained a quiet settlement, but in 1821, Mexico gained independence from Spain, and California became part of Mexico. This period brought new changes to Old Town, as Mexican ranchers and traders arrived, building larger homes and starting businesses. The town became a lively place, with fiestas, music, and celebrations filling the streets. Mexican culture left a lasting impact on Old Town, which can still be seen in the colorful decorations, traditional Mexican restaurants, and historic buildings that remain today.

In 1848, after the Mexican-American War, California became part of the United States. This change brought even more settlers, including pioneers, merchants, and adventurers looking for new opportunities. The 1850s were an exciting time for Old Town as more businesses opened, schools were built, and the population grew. One of the most famous figures from this time was Juan Bandini, a wealthy rancher whose home, Casa de Bandini, became a center for social gatherings, dances, and political meetings. Today, visitors can still see this historic house, which has been turned into a museum and restaurant, preserving the rich history of the era.

One of the most interesting buildings in Old Town is the Whaley House, which is considered one of the most haunted houses in America. Built in the 1850s by Thomas Whaley, this house served as a family home, a store, and even a courthouse. Over the years, people have reported seeing ghosts and hearing strange noises inside. Some say the spirits of early settlers, criminals, and even members of the Whaley family still roam the house. Whether you believe in ghosts or not, the Whaley House is an important part of Old Town's history and a fascinating place to visit.

Another famous landmark is the Old Town San Diego State Historic Park, which preserves many original buildings from the 1800s. Walking through this park is like traveling back in time, as visitors can see blacksmith shops, old-fashioned general stores, and historic homes decorated just as they were in the past. There are costumed reenactors who demonstrate how people lived, worked, and dressed in the 19th century. You might see a blacksmith shaping iron, a shopkeeper selling goods, or a musician playing traditional Mexican songs. These experiences help bring history to life and make Old Town an exciting place to learn about the past.

One of the best ways to experience Old Town is by visiting the historic restaurants and tasting the delicious food. Many of the restaurants serve traditional Mexican dishes like tacos, enchiladas, tamales, and fresh tortillas made right in front of you. Some of the oldest restaurants have been serving food for decades, giving visitors a taste of the flavors that have been enjoyed for generations. The lively atmosphere, with mariachi bands playing music and people celebrating, makes dining in Old Town a fun and memorable experience.

Old Town is also home to several fascinating museums that showcase different parts of San Diego's history. The Mormon Battalion Historic Site tells the story of a group of Mormon pioneers who marched thousands of miles to help build San Diego in the 1840s. The Wells Fargo Museum shows how stagecoaches and banking played an important role in the city's development. The Robinson-Rose House, once the headquarters of an early newspaper, now serves as a visitor center where people can learn more about Old Town's history.

Throughout the year, Old Town hosts many festivals and special events that celebrate its rich cultural heritage. Día de los Muertos, or Day of the Dead, is one of the most popular celebrations, where families honor their ancestors with colorful altars, decorations, and parades. Cinco de Mayo is another exciting event, filled with music, dancing, and delicious food. During Christmas, Old Town is beautifully decorated with lights, and traditional holiday celebrations take place, bringing history and culture together in a festive way.

Even though San Diego has grown into a modern city with tall buildings, highways, and new neighborhoods, Old Town remains a special place where the past is still alive. Every street, building, and artifact has a story to tell, reminding visitors of the people who once walked these same paths hundreds of years ago. Whether you're exploring a historic home, listening to the sounds of a mariachi band, or tasting authentic Mexican food, Old Town offers a glimpse into the history that shaped San Diego.

Visiting Old Town is like stepping into a living museum where history, culture, and tradition blend together. It's a place where kids and adults can learn in a fun and interactive way, experiencing what life was like in the past while enjoying all the excitement the area has to offer. With so many historic sites, museums, restaurants, and events, Old Town San Diego is truly a treasure that keeps history alive for future generations to discover and enjoy.

Chapter 5: The Wonders of SeaWorld

SeaWorld San Diego is one of the most exciting places to visit in the city, especially for kids and families who love marine life, thrilling rides, and incredible shows. It is a huge ocean-themed park filled with amazing sea creatures, educational exhibits, and fun attractions that allow visitors to get up close to some of the most fascinating animals that live in the ocean. Whether you want to see playful dolphins, watch massive orcas leap out of the water, or experience the rush of high-speed roller coasters, SeaWorld has something for everyone.

One of the main attractions at SeaWorld is the chance to see marine animals that you might never get to see in the wild. The park is home to a variety of sea creatures, including orcas, dolphins, sea lions, otters, sharks, rays, penguins, and colorful fish. Walking through the park feels like stepping into an underwater world, where every turn leads to a new and exciting discovery. Some of the exhibits allow visitors to touch certain animals, while others provide a close-up view of marine life in habitats designed to mimic the ocean.

The orcas, also known as killer whales, are some of the most famous animals at SeaWorld. These powerful black-and-white marine mammals are known for their intelligence, social behavior, and incredible acrobatics. At SeaWorld, visitors can watch orcas perform amazing tricks, such as jumping high out of the water, spinning in the air, and splashing the audience with huge waves. The trainers work closely with these majestic animals, teaching them different behaviors and rewarding them with fish. Seeing an orca up close is an unforgettable experience because of their size and grace. They can weigh as much as a school bus and move effortlessly through the water, making them one of the most impressive sights in the park.

Dolphins are another crowd favorite at SeaWorld. These playful and intelligent creatures love to interact with people and can be seen leaping, spinning, and swimming in synchronized routines. One of the most exciting parts of the dolphin experience is watching how they communicate with their trainers using clicks, whistles, and body movements. Some lucky visitors even get the chance to feed or touch a dolphin, making it a magical experience. Dolphins are known for their friendly nature, and at SeaWorld, guests can learn all about their behavior, diet, and natural habitat.

Sea lions and otters are also popular animals at the park. The sea lion shows are both funny and entertaining, as these playful animals perform tricks, clap their flippers, and even pretend to "talk" to their trainers. The otters, on the other hand, are small and energetic, often seen floating on their backs while holding food or playing with toys. Watching these animals is a great way to learn about marine mammals and how they survive in the wild.

For those who love sharks, SeaWorld has an incredible shark exhibit that takes visitors through an underwater tunnel surrounded by some of the ocean's most powerful predators. Walking through the tunnel feels like being inside the ocean, with sharks swimming overhead and around you. Some sharks are small, while others are huge and look like they came straight out of a prehistoric world. This exhibit helps people understand more about sharks, how they hunt, and why they are important for keeping the ocean ecosystem balanced.

The touch pools at SeaWorld allow visitors to interact with some of the friendliest creatures of the ocean. In these special areas, people can gently touch stingrays as they glide through the water, feel the rough shells of sea stars, or watch small fish swim between their fingers. This hands-on experience is perfect for kids who love to explore and learn about ocean life in a fun and interactive way.

In addition to animal exhibits, SeaWorld is also famous for its thrilling rides and attractions. The park has roller coasters, water rides, and interactive experiences that add even more excitement to the visit. One of the most popular rides is the Emperor, a dive coaster that drops riders from a height of over 150 feet at a nearly vertical angle.

This heart-pounding ride is perfect for those who love extreme thrills. Another exciting roller coaster is the Electric Eel, which twists, loops, and speeds through the air at high speeds, giving riders the sensation of flying over the ocean.

For families looking for a more relaxed ride, Journey to Atlantis combines a boat ride with a roller coaster experience, taking guests through ancient ruins before plunging them into the water with a giant splash. There is also Shipwreck Rapids, a fun water raft ride that takes passengers through waterfalls, rapids, and swirling currents, making it the perfect way to cool off on a hot day.

Younger kids can enjoy rides like the Sea Dragon Drop, a mini free-fall ride, or the Sesame Street Bay of Play, which has smaller rides, splash areas, and playgrounds featuring beloved Sesame Street characters. This area is perfect for little ones who might not be ready for the big roller coasters but still want to have fun.

One of the best things about SeaWorld is that it is not just about entertainment; it is also dedicated to education and conservation. The park plays an important role in rescuing and rehabilitating marine animals that are sick, injured, or stranded. Over the years, SeaWorld's rescue teams have helped thousands of animals, including sea lions, dolphins, turtles, and seabirds. Many of these animals are released back into the wild after they recover, helping to protect marine life and keep the ocean healthy.

Throughout the park, there are interactive exhibits and presentations that teach visitors about the importance of protecting the environment. Shows and displays explain how pollution, climate change, and overfishing affect ocean life and what people can do to help. Guests can learn about efforts to clean up beaches, reduce plastic waste, and protect endangered species. SeaWorld encourages people to respect and care for the ocean, inspiring future generations to become marine conservationists.

During different times of the year, SeaWorld also hosts special events and seasonal celebrations. During Halloween, the park transforms into a spooky but fun experience with trick-or-treating, costume contests, and special shows. At Christmas, the park is filled with holiday lights, decorations, and even snowfall in certain areas. One of the most exciting events is the summer fireworks show, where bright colors light up the night sky over the ocean, making for a perfect ending to an adventurous day at SeaWorld.

Food lovers will also find plenty of delicious options at SeaWorld. The park offers a variety of meals, from fresh seafood and burgers to tasty snacks like funnel cakes and ice cream. There are also themed dining experiences, such as eating near the shark exhibit or enjoying a meal while watching dolphins play in the water. Many of the restaurants use ocean-friendly practices, such as serving sustainable seafood, which helps protect marine life.

With so much to see and do, a visit to SeaWorld can be a full-day adventure filled with unforgettable experiences. Whether you are learning about the amazing creatures of the ocean, riding an exciting roller coaster, or watching a breathtaking animal show, there is always something new to discover. The combination of fun, education, and conservation makes SeaWorld one of the most unique attractions in San Diego. It is a place where people of all ages can connect with the wonders of the sea, gain a deeper appreciation for marine life, and create memories that will last a lifetime.

Chapter 6: A Day at Mission Bay

Mission Bay is one of the most exciting and beautiful places in San Diego, where visitors can spend an entire day enjoying the sunshine, water, and endless outdoor activities. It is the largest man-made aquatic park in the United States, covering over 4,600 acres of land and water, with miles of sandy beaches, peaceful lagoons, and scenic bike paths. Whether you love swimming, sailing, kayaking, paddleboarding, biking, or just relaxing on the shore, Mission Bay has something for everyone. Families, friends, and nature lovers can all find something to enjoy in this massive waterfront playground, making it the perfect destination for an unforgettable day of fun and adventure.

A day at Mission Bay often starts in the early morning when the air is cool, the water is calm, and the park is just beginning to wake up. Many people start their visit with a peaceful walk or bike ride along the scenic paths that stretch for miles around the bay. The bike trails wind past sandy beaches, grassy parks, and marinas filled with boats, offering breathtaking views of the water and the surrounding city. Early in the morning, you might see joggers, rollerbladers, and people walking their dogs, enjoying the fresh air and quiet beauty of the bay. The calm waters also make it a perfect time for paddleboarders and kayakers, who gently glide across the smooth surface of the bay, taking in the peaceful scenery before the day gets busy.

As the sun rises higher, more people begin to arrive, ready to enjoy the warm sand and cool water. The beaches of Mission Bay are perfect for families, with soft sand for building sandcastles, gentle waves for wading, and plenty of open space for beach games like volleyball or frisbee. Kids love splashing in the shallow water, digging in the sand, and searching for seashells along the shore. Some beaches have playgrounds nearby, where children can climb, swing, and slide while parents relax on picnic benches under shady trees.

For those who love water sports, Mission Bay is a paradise. Jet skis zip across the water, leaving behind white trails of foam, while sailboats glide gracefully, their sails catching the ocean breeze. Many people rent kayaks or stand-up paddleboards to explore the bay at their own pace, paddling past small islands, under bridges, and alongside birds that float gently on the water. One of the most popular activities is renting a pedal boat, which allows families and friends to cruise the bay together while enjoying the sunshine.

Boating is another huge part of the Mission Bay experience. Visitors can rent motorboats, speedboats, or even larger pontoon boats for a fun day on the water. Some people bring their own boats and launch them from the many ramps around the bay, while others take guided boat tours that offer a relaxing way to explore the area. For those who love fishing, Mission Bay is a great place to cast a line and try to catch fish like halibut, bass, and mackerel. Many people enjoy fishing from the piers or even from their boats, hoping to reel in a big catch.

Lunch at Mission Bay is often a delicious picnic enjoyed at one of the many grassy parks with picnic tables and barbecue grills. Families and friends gather under the shade of large trees to enjoy sandwiches, grilled burgers, fresh fruit, and cold drinks while watching the boats go by. Some visitors bring coolers filled with snacks and drinks, while others stop by nearby food stands or restaurants to grab a tasty meal. With so many beautiful spots to sit and eat, every meal at Mission Bay feels like a special occasion.

In the afternoon, the bay becomes even more lively as more people arrive to enjoy the water and sunshine. Some visitors rent beach cruisers and ride along the paths that stretch around the bay, feeling the breeze on their faces as they pass by parks, marinas, and sparkling water. Others set up beach umbrellas and towels to relax and soak up the sun while listening to the sound of gentle waves. Kids love playing in the water, splashing, swimming, and floating on inflatable rafts or boogie boards. The bay's calm waters make it a great place to practice swimming or just float lazily without worrying about big waves.

Adventure seekers can try wakeboarding or water skiing, where they hold onto a rope and glide across the water at high speed, jumping over waves and performing tricks. For those who prefer something a little more relaxing, there are guided kayak tours that take visitors around the bay, explaining the history, wildlife, and special features of this amazing area. One of the highlights of Mission Bay is its wildlife—many birds, fish, and even sea lions can be spotted throughout the day, making it a great place for nature lovers.

As the day moves toward evening, people start gathering at the fire pits scattered around the bay. These fire pits are perfect for roasting marshmallows, making s'mores, and telling stories as the sun begins to set over the water. The sky turns shades of orange, pink, and purple, creating a breathtaking view that makes the perfect ending to a fun-filled day. Many families and groups of friends bring blankets and folding chairs, settling in to watch the sunset while enjoying the cool evening breeze.

At night, Mission Bay takes on a magical atmosphere. Some boats have colorful lights that reflect on the water, while others drift quietly under the stars. The sound of laughter, music, and the crackling of beach bonfires fills the air, creating a cozy and joyful feeling. Nighttime boat cruises offer a unique way to experience the bay, as passengers glide over the calm water while enjoying the city lights in the distance.

For those who aren't ready for the day to end, there are even campsites near the bay where people can stay overnight. Camping near the water allows visitors to wake up to the sound of gentle waves and enjoy another beautiful day of adventure. Many families and groups set up tents, cook meals over campfires, and tell stories under the stars, making memories that last a lifetime.

Mission Bay is more than just a place to swim and sunbathe—it is a true outdoor paradise filled with exciting activities, natural beauty, and endless opportunities for fun. Whether you're spending the day paddleboarding, having a picnic, riding bikes, or simply relaxing on the beach, there's always something to do. The combination of land and water activities makes it one of the best places in San Diego for a perfect day outdoors. No matter how many times you visit, there is always something new to discover, and every trip to Mission Bay feels like a special adventure.

Chapter 7: Wildlife at Safari Park

San Diego Zoo Safari Park is one of the most exciting places in California to see animals up close and experience the thrill of a safari adventure without leaving the United States. Located in Escondido, just north of San Diego, this massive wildlife park covers over 1,800 acres of land, providing a home for thousands of animals from all over the world. Unlike traditional zoos, the Safari Park is designed to give animals large, open spaces that closely resemble their natural habitats. This means that visitors get to see animals roaming freely across vast grasslands, just as they would in the wild. From towering giraffes and mighty rhinos to playful cheetahs and colorful birds, every corner of the park is filled with incredible creatures, making it a dream destination for animal lovers and adventure seekers.

One of the most exciting things about the Safari Park is its wide variety of animals. The park is home to more than 3,000 animals representing over 300 different species. Some of the most famous animals here are the African and Asian elephants, which can be seen strolling through their spacious habitat, flapping their ears and using their trunks to grab food and water. Watching elephants interact is fascinating—they are intelligent, social animals that communicate with each other using deep rumbles and body language. Visitors often see them splashing in the water, playing in the dirt, or using their trunks to reach for tasty treats.

Another highlight of the park is the large herds of giraffes that gracefully walk across the open savanna. Giraffes are the tallest animals on Earth, and seeing them up close is an unforgettable experience. At the Safari Park, visitors can even get the chance to feed a giraffe by holding out a piece of lettuce or acacia leaves. The giraffes gently extend their long, purple tongues to grab the food, making for an exciting and memorable moment. Because giraffes are naturally curious, they often come right up to the safari trucks, giving visitors a close-up look at their big, dark eyes and beautiful spotted coats.

One of the most thrilling parts of the park is the African Plains exhibit, a massive area designed to look like the open grasslands of Africa. Here, animals such as zebras, rhinos, antelopes, and gazelles live together in a setting that looks just like their natural environment. Zebras, with their striking black-and-white stripes, are always a favorite to watch. Each zebra has a unique pattern, just like human fingerprints, which helps them recognize each other. Nearby, rhinos roam across the fields, sometimes rolling in the mud to cool off and protect their thick skin from the sun. The Safari Park has played an important role in protecting rhinos, helping to breed and care for these incredible animals, especially since many species of rhinos are endangered in the wild.

Cheetahs are another exciting species that visitors can see at the park. These sleek, spotted cats are the fastest land animals on Earth, capable of reaching speeds up to 70 miles per hour in just a few seconds. One of the most unique things about the Safari Park is the cheetah run, where visitors can watch a cheetah sprint at full speed across a special track. Seeing a cheetah move so fast is breathtaking—its long legs stretch out in powerful strides, and its flexible spine allows it to cover huge distances in just a few steps. Cheetahs at the park often have special companions: trained dogs that help keep them calm. These cheetah-dog friendships are part of a special program that helps cheetahs feel more relaxed and comfortable in their environment.

The Safari Park is also home to many amazing birds. The park's aviaries are filled with colorful species, from bright pink flamingos to massive Andean condors with wingspans reaching over 10 feet. Flamingos are especially fun to watch as they wade through the water, dipping their curved beaks to scoop up tiny shrimp and algae. Their bright pink color comes from the food they eat, and young flamingos start out gray before turning pink as they grow. In another part of the park, visitors can see majestic eagles, owls, and hawks, some of which participate in special bird shows where they swoop down from the sky and display their incredible hunting skills.

One of the most adventurous ways to explore the park is by taking the Africa Tram, an open-air safari ride that takes visitors through the heart of the African Plains. As the tram rolls through the landscape, visitors get the chance to see animals just as they would in the wild—giraffes stretching their long necks to nibble on tree leaves, rhinos taking mud baths, and herds of gazelles gracefully leaping across the fields. The tram ride is a great way to see many animals in a short amount of time while also learning interesting facts about each species from the guide.

Another way to experience the park is through the special behind-the-scenes tours and safari adventures. Some tours allow visitors to ride in open safari trucks that take them right into the middle of the animal habitats, where they can get closer than ever to rhinos, giraffes, and other incredible creatures. Other tours offer the chance to see how the park's animal experts care for the animals, including feeding sessions, training demonstrations, and even baby animal nurseries where young animals receive special care.

In addition to the larger animals, the Safari Park is home to many smaller but equally fascinating creatures. Meerkats, with their curious faces and playful personalities, can often be seen standing on their hind legs, scanning the area for danger. These tiny mammals live in groups and take turns keeping watch while the rest of the group digs tunnels or searches for food. Warthogs, which may not be the prettiest animals, are fun to watch as they trot around with their stiff tails pointing straight up in the air. Lemurs, native to Madagascar, are another highlight, with their bright eyes and long, bushy tails that help them balance as they leap from tree to tree.

The Safari Park is not just about seeing animals—it is also dedicated to protecting them. The park is involved in many conservation projects to help endangered species and protect wildlife around the world. Scientists and veterinarians at the park work on breeding programs to save rare animals, such as the northern white rhino, which is one of the most endangered species on Earth. The park also helps rescue injured animals, cares for orphaned baby animals, and works with conservationists in other countries to protect wild habitats.

As the sun begins to set over the park, the animals start to wind down for the evening. Some animals, like lions, become more active at dusk, roaring and stretching after a long day of resting in the shade. Others, like elephants, gather in small groups, gently touching trunks as a way to bond before settling in for the night. The park takes on a peaceful, golden glow as visitors make their way to the exits, reflecting on the amazing sights they've seen and the unforgettable experiences they've had.

A visit to San Diego Zoo Safari Park is more than just a trip to see animals—it is an adventure into the wild, a chance to witness the beauty of nature, and an opportunity to learn about the importance of protecting wildlife for future generations. With so many incredible animals, exciting safari rides, and breathtaking landscapes, every visit feels like a journey to another world, filled with wonder, discovery, and excitement.

Chapter 8: Adventures on Coronado Island

Coronado Island is a magical place just across the bay from downtown San Diego, and visiting it feels like stepping into a completely different world. Even though it is called an island, it is actually a peninsula connected to the mainland by a long stretch of land known as the Silver Strand. Coronado is famous for its beautiful beaches, historic buildings, charming small-town feel, and breathtaking views of the Pacific Ocean. Whether visitors arrive by car, ferry, or even bicycle, there is always something exciting to explore. From golden sandy beaches and historic landmarks to outdoor adventures and delicious food, Coronado Island is packed with fun for the whole family.

One of the best ways to begin an adventure on Coronado is by taking the ferry from downtown San Diego. The ride itself is an exciting experience, as it offers stunning views of the San Diego skyline, the busy harbor, and even naval ships docked nearby. As the ferry glides across the sparkling water, seagulls soar overhead, and if you're lucky, you might even spot a playful dolphin swimming alongside the boat. The ferry arrives at the Coronado Ferry Landing, a charming waterfront area filled with shops, restaurants, and places to rent bikes or kayaks. From here, visitors can start exploring the island in many different ways.

One of the most famous landmarks on Coronado Island is the legendary Hotel del Coronado, often called "The Del." This grand hotel, built in 1888, looks like a fairy-tale castle with its red rooftops, white wooden walls, and elegant towers. Over the years, it has welcomed many famous guests, including presidents, movie stars, and even royalty. Walking through the hotel feels like stepping back in time, as it is filled with vintage charm, beautiful chandeliers, and stories of the past. Some people even believe that the hotel is haunted by the ghost of a mysterious woman named Kate Morgan, who checked into the hotel in 1892 and never checked out. Many visitors enjoy exploring the hallways, visiting the small museum inside, and learning about the rich history of this iconic building.

Beyond the hotel, one of the biggest highlights of Coronado is its incredible beaches. Coronado Beach is often ranked as one of the best beaches in the United States, and for a good reason. The sand here is special—it contains tiny flakes of mica, a mineral that makes the beach shimmer in the sunlight. This gives the sand a golden, almost magical glow, which is why many people call it the "Silver Strand." The beach stretches for miles, offering plenty of space for families to spread out, build sandcastles, and splash in the gentle waves. The water is usually calm, making it perfect for swimming, boogie boarding, and even stand-up paddleboarding. On some days, skilled surfers can be seen riding the waves, balancing effortlessly on their boards as they glide across the ocean.

For those who love adventure, renting a bike is one of the best ways to see more of Coronado. There are many bike paths around the island, including one that runs along the waterfront, offering stunning views of the bay, the city skyline, and passing sailboats. Tandem bikes, which allow two people to ride together, are a fun option for families, while surreys—four-wheeled pedal-powered carts—are perfect for groups who want to ride together in style. Riding through the island, visitors can explore beautiful neighborhoods filled with charming houses, colorful gardens, and towering palm trees swaying in the breeze. Many of the homes have a unique story, and some have been standing for over a hundred years, giving Coronado a timeless, picture-perfect feel.

Another great way to experience Coronado is by heading to Tidelands Park, a peaceful waterfront area with grassy fields, picnic spots, and incredible views of the Coronado Bridge. This massive blue bridge stretches high above the bay, curving gracefully as it connects San Diego to Coronado. It is an impressive sight, especially at sunrise or sunset when the sky is painted in shades of orange, pink, and purple. At Tidelands Park, kids can run around on the playground, families can enjoy a picnic by the water, and people can often be seen jogging, rollerblading, or simply relaxing in the sunshine. Kayaking and paddleboarding are also popular activities here, as the calm bay waters make it easy for beginners to enjoy a fun and peaceful ride.

For those interested in history, a visit to the Coronado Historical Association Museum is a great way to learn more about the island's fascinating past. The museum showcases old photographs, artifacts, and exhibits about the early days of Coronado, including its role as a military base and a playground for the rich and famous. The museum also highlights stories of the U.S. Navy, which has a strong presence on the island. Coronado is home to Naval Air Station North Island, where aircraft carriers, helicopters, and military planes can often be seen. In fact, North Island is known as the "Birthplace of Naval Aviation" because it was one of the first places where pilots were trained to fly for the U.S. Navy. Sometimes, visitors can spot naval aircraft taking off and landing, adding a thrilling sight to the island's atmosphere.

Food lovers will also find plenty of delicious options on Coronado. The island has many great restaurants, cafés, and ice cream shops, offering everything from fresh seafood to tasty tacos. Many visitors love trying fish tacos, a local favorite made with crispy fish, tangy sauce, and fresh toppings wrapped in a warm tortilla. For dessert, a stop at one of the island's famous ice cream parlors is a must. With flavors ranging from classic chocolate and vanilla to unique options like lavender honey and Mexican chocolate, there's something for everyone to enjoy. Eating ice cream while strolling along the beach or watching the boats in the bay is the perfect way to end a fun-filled day.

As the sun begins to set, Coronado takes on a magical glow. The beach becomes a peaceful paradise as the sky turns golden, and gentle waves roll onto the shore. People gather on the sand to watch the sunset, taking photos and enjoying the cool ocean breeze. Some visitors choose to stay late to see the twinkling city lights of San Diego reflecting on the water, creating a stunning nighttime view. Others take the ferry back to downtown, enjoying one last breathtaking ride across the bay before heading home.

A trip to Coronado Island is truly an unforgettable experience. Whether spending the day relaxing on the beach, biking through charming streets, exploring historic landmarks, or enjoying delicious food, there is always something exciting to discover. With its perfect blend of natural beauty, rich history, and fun activities, Coronado is a place that captures the heart of every visitor. Each adventure on the island creates lasting memories, making it a destination that people want to return to again and again.

Chapter 9: Discovering Little Italy

Little Italy in San Diego is one of the most exciting and vibrant neighborhoods in the city, full of history, culture, delicious food, and lively streets that make it a favorite spot for both locals and visitors. Walking through this charming district feels like stepping into a different world, where the smell of freshly baked bread and simmering pasta fills the air, music drifts from street cafés, and colorful murals decorate the buildings. With its rich Italian heritage, bustling farmers' markets, and incredible restaurants, Little Italy is a place where the past and present blend perfectly, offering something for everyone to enjoy.

Long ago, before Little Italy became the popular destination it is today, it was home to a hardworking community of Italian immigrants who came to San Diego in the late 19th and early 20th centuries. Many of these families were fishermen who settled in the area because of its close connection to the bay. They built small houses, set up businesses, and formed a close-knit neighborhood where everyone knew each other. Fishing was the heart of the community, and the waters of San Diego Bay were filled with boats that belonged to Italian fishermen. These families worked hard to supply the city with fresh seafood, especially tuna, which became one of San Diego's biggest industries. Because of their dedication and skill, San Diego earned the nickname "The Tuna Capital of the World."

Over time, the fishing industry changed, and many families moved on to other jobs, but the spirit of Little Italy remained strong. Today, the neighborhood is filled with beautiful Italian restaurants, specialty shops, art galleries, and lively events that celebrate its cultural roots. One of the best ways to explore Little Italy is simply by walking down India Street, the main road that runs through the district. Here, visitors can find everything from cozy cafés and pizzerias to high-end Italian restaurants serving gourmet dishes. Many of these eateries have been owned by Italian families for generations, and some even have recipes that have been passed down for over a hundred years!

One of the biggest attractions in Little Italy is the Mercato Farmers' Market, which happens every Saturday morning. It is the largest farmers' market in San Diego, stretching across several blocks and filled with over 200 vendors selling fresh fruits, vegetables, handmade crafts, delicious food, and more. Walking through the market is a feast for the senses, with the bright colors of ripe produce, the smell of fresh flowers, and the sounds of musicians playing lively tunes. People come from all over the city to buy farm-fresh goods, sample tasty treats, and enjoy the friendly, welcoming atmosphere.

Another highlight of Little Italy is the amazing food. No visit to the neighborhood is complete without trying some classic Italian dishes like homemade pasta, wood-fired pizza, and creamy gelato. Many restaurants make their pasta from scratch every day, rolling out sheets of dough and cutting it into perfect strands of spaghetti, fettuccine, or ravioli. Pizzerias cook their pizzas in giant stone ovens, creating crispy crusts topped with fresh tomato sauce, mozzarella cheese, and flavorful toppings like basil, mushrooms, and Italian sausage. And of course, no meal is complete without dessert! Gelato, a creamy Italian-style ice cream, comes in all sorts of flavors, from rich chocolate and vanilla to fruity options like mango and strawberry.

Beyond the food, Little Italy is also a place where art and culture thrive. Walking through the streets, visitors can spot beautiful murals painted on the sides of buildings, each telling a unique story about the neighborhood's history and people. Some murals show scenes of Italian fishermen bringing in their catch, while others feature famous Italian landmarks or traditional designs. There are also many art galleries showcasing the work of talented local artists, from paintings and sculptures to handmade jewelry and pottery.

One of the most famous landmarks in Little Italy is Piazza della Famiglia, a beautiful open plaza where people gather to eat, relax, and enjoy live entertainment. This European-style square is decorated with string lights, fountains, and comfortable seating, making it the perfect spot to sit with a slice of pizza or a cup of coffee and watch the world go by. Throughout the year, Piazza della Famiglia hosts special events like concerts, holiday celebrations, and outdoor movie nights, bringing the community together in a fun and festive way.

Little Italy also comes alive during festivals, especially the annual Festa, which celebrates Italian culture with food, music, and performances. During this event, the streets are filled with food stalls selling everything from fresh pasta to cannoli, a delicious Italian pastry filled with sweet ricotta cheese. Live bands play Italian folk music, dancers perform traditional routines, and artists set up booths to display their work. Another popular event is the Little Italy Carnevale, a colorful festival inspired by the famous Venetian Carnival in Italy, where people dress in masks and costumes, adding an extra touch of magic to the neighborhood.

For those who love exploring hidden gems, Little Italy has plenty of unique shops to discover. Specialty grocery stores sell imported Italian cheeses, olive oils, and handmade pasta, allowing visitors to take a taste of Italy home with them. Bakeries fill their shelves with freshly baked bread, biscotti, and pastries, while boutique clothing stores offer stylish fashion inspired by Italian trends. Even if someone isn't looking to buy anything, simply browsing through the shops and taking in the sights and smells is an enjoyable experience.

As the sun sets, Little Italy takes on a whole new charm. The twinkling lights strung above the streets create a warm, inviting glow, and the outdoor patios of restaurants fill with people enjoying delicious meals under the stars. Musicians often perform live on the sidewalks, adding a lively soundtrack to the evening. Couples stroll hand in hand, friends gather to share plates of pasta, and families enjoy laughter-filled dinners together. The energy of the neighborhood is contagious, making it impossible not to smile and soak in the happiness of the moment.

Even though it has changed over the years, Little Italy has never lost its sense of community and tradition. It remains a place where history is honored, where food is made with love, and where people from all backgrounds come together to enjoy the simple joys of life. Whether visiting for a few hours or spending the whole day, Little Italy always leaves a lasting impression. From the mouthwatering food and colorful markets to the rich history and warm atmosphere, it is a place that captures the heart and keeps visitors coming back for more.

Chapter 10: Fun at LEGOLAND

LEGOLAND California is one of the most exciting places to visit in San Diego, especially for kids and families who love adventure, creativity, and, of course, LEGO bricks! Located in Carlsbad, just north of San Diego, this amazing theme park is a dreamland filled with thrilling rides, interactive attractions, and stunning LEGO creations that bring imagination to life. Walking through the gates of LEGOLAND feels like stepping into a giant LEGO world where everything is colorful, playful, and designed to spark fun. From roller coasters and water rides to life-sized LEGO sculptures and hands-on building zones, every part of the park is filled with excitement, making it a must-visit destination for LEGO fans of all ages.

One of the first things that visitors see when they enter LEGOLAND is the huge LEGO-themed entrance, which immediately sets the tone for an incredible adventure. Right away, guests are surrounded by massive LEGO figures, cool designs, and fun surprises hidden around every corner. It's easy to feel like a mini-figure inside a LEGO set because everything is built to resemble the famous bricks. There are over 60 rides, attractions, and shows spread throughout the park, ensuring that there's never a dull moment.

One of the biggest highlights of LEGOLAND is Miniland USA, a section of the park where famous cities and landmarks are recreated using millions of tiny LEGO bricks. Here, visitors can marvel at miniature versions of real-life places, including San Francisco, New York City, Las Vegas, and even San Diego itself! The level of detail is truly incredible—tiny LEGO people walk the streets, LEGO cars drive on highways, and some of the buildings even have moving parts, like boats sailing through the waterways or trains traveling along the tracks. Visitors can spend hours exploring Miniland, spotting hidden details, and watching as special LEGO scenes come to life with lights, music, and motion.

For those who love thrilling rides, LEGOLAND has plenty of options. One of the most exciting rides is The Dragon, a roller coaster that takes guests on a fun journey through a LEGO castle filled with knights, wizards, and fire-breathing dragons before speeding through twists and turns outside. Another popular attraction is Coastersaurus, a dinosaur-themed roller coaster that zips through a prehistoric LEGO jungle where brick-built dinosaurs stand tall. Kids who want to take control of their own adventure can hop on Driving School, where they get to drive mini LEGO cars on a real road with stop signs, intersections, and even traffic lights! For those who love water, Splash Battle is a great ride where guests climb aboard pirate ships and spray water cannons at targets—and sometimes at each other!

One of the unique things about LEGOLAND is that it's designed to be hands-on, meaning visitors don't just look at cool LEGO builds—they get to create their own! In areas like Build & Test, kids can design and build their own LEGO cars, then race them down tracks to see how fast they go. At the LEGO Mindstorms zone, kids can program and control real LEGO robots, learning about technology and engineering in a fun and interactive way. Another creative spot is the Imagination Zone, where guests can use their building skills to make towers, bridges, or even entire LEGO cities. There's even a chance to build and test LEGO boats, racing them down water-filled tracks to see whose creation floats the fastest.

For fans of LEGO movies, there are special sections of the park dedicated to some of the most popular LEGO characters and stories. One of the most exciting areas is LEGO Ninjago World, where visitors can train like real ninjas and test their skills in an awesome interactive ride called Ninjago The Ride. This ride uses motion-sensing technology that lets guests use their hands to throw fireballs, lightning, and ice at enemies on the screen, just like real ninjas! Another movie-inspired attraction is The LEGO Movie World, where guests can step into the world of Emmet, Wyldstyle, and Batman. The area includes fun rides like Emmet's Flying Adventure, which takes visitors on a thrilling 3D journey through the LEGO Movie universe.

For those visiting on a hot day, LEGOLAND also has an amazing water park filled with slides, splash zones, and lazy rivers. The LEGO-themed water park is packed with fun attractions, including Build-A-Raft River, where visitors can design and build their own floating rafts using giant LEGO bricks before floating down a winding waterway. There's also the Joker Soaker, a massive play structure with slides, climbing areas, and a giant bucket that dumps water on everyone below. Kids who love slides can race down the Twin Chasers or take a wild ride through the Red Rush, a huge water slide built for families to enjoy together.

One of the most exciting parts of LEGOLAND is the SEA LIFE Aquarium, an incredible underwater world filled with fascinating sea creatures. Unlike regular aquariums, this one includes LEGO models inside the tanks, creating a unique mix of real marine life and playful LEGO designs. Visitors can see sharks, rays, jellyfish, and even sea turtles while walking through tunnels and looking into beautifully designed exhibits. There are also interactive touch pools where kids can get up close with sea stars, sea urchins, and other gentle ocean creatures. The combination of marine education and LEGO creativity makes this aquarium a special experience unlike any other.

LEGOLAND isn't just about rides and attractions—it also has tons of live entertainment and special events throughout the year. Guests can watch live stunt shows, 4D LEGO movies, and musical performances featuring their favorite LEGO characters. During Halloween, the park hosts Brick-or-Treat, a spooky but fun event where kids can dress up in costumes, go trick-or-treating around the park, and enjoy special Halloween-themed activities. During the holiday season, LEGOLAND transforms into a winter wonderland, complete with giant LEGO Christmas trees, holiday decorations, and even a LEGO Santa Claus!

Of course, no trip to LEGOLAND is complete without checking out the amazing LEGO shops and restaurants. The park has several stores selling LEGO sets, rare mini-figures, and exclusive items that can't be found anywhere else. One of the most popular stops is the Minifigure Market, where guests can create their own custom LEGO mini-figures by mixing and matching different heads, bodies, and accessories. When it's time to eat, LEGOLAND offers a variety of fun and tasty food options, including giant LEGO-shaped waffles, brick-themed burgers, and delicious pizza.

At the end of an action-packed day, visitors often leave LEGOLAND with big smiles, full of excitement from all the fun they had. Whether building their own creations, meeting LEGO characters, or zooming down thrilling rides, there's always something new to explore. LEGOLAND is a place where creativity and adventure come together, allowing kids and families to step into a world built entirely out of imagination. Every visit brings new surprises, making it a destination that people love to return to again and again.

Chapter 11: Ships and Stories at Maritime Museum

The Maritime Museum of San Diego is one of the most fascinating places to visit for anyone who loves ships, history, and tales of the sea. This incredible museum isn't like a regular museum where you walk through halls looking at glass cases and paintings. Instead, it's a floating museum, meaning all of its exhibits are real ships! Docked along the waterfront in downtown San Diego, this museum gives visitors the rare opportunity to step aboard historic vessels, explore their decks, and imagine what life was like for sailors, explorers, and even pirates from long ago. With a collection of some of the most well-preserved historic ships in the world, the Maritime Museum is a place full of adventure, discovery, and stories from the past.

One of the most famous ships in the museum's collection is the *Star of India*, the world's oldest active sailing ship. This majestic vessel was built in 1863, during the time of wooden ships and tall sails, and has traveled around the world multiple times. When visitors step onto the *Star of India*, they feel like they've traveled back in time. The ship's creaky wooden decks, towering masts, and massive ropes give a glimpse of what life was like for sailors who worked tirelessly at sea. This ship was once used to carry goods, immigrants, and supplies across vast oceans. During its long history, it faced dangerous storms, survived rough waters, and even played a role in trade between Europe and the Pacific. Walking through its cabins, visitors can see the cramped spaces where sailors slept, the galley where meals were prepared, and the captain's quarters, which were much fancier than the rest of the ship. It's amazing to think that this ship is still seaworthy today, and on special occasions, it even sets sail!

Another exciting ship in the museum's collection is the *HMS Surprise*, a beautiful replica of a British Royal Navy frigate from the

18th century. If this ship looks familiar, it's because it was used in the Hollywood movie *Master and Commander: The Far Side of the World*, starring Russell Crowe. The *HMS Surprise* is a perfect example of the type of ships that sailed during the Age of Exploration and the Napoleonic Wars. Its wooden cannons, detailed rigging, and classic design make visitors feel like they've stepped into an old pirate or naval adventure. The ship is so realistic that when walking across its deck, visitors can almost hear the sounds of sailors shouting commands, the wind whipping through the sails, and the distant crash of waves against the hull. This ship helps people understand what life was like for naval officers and sailors who spent months, or even years, out at sea.

One of the most eye-catching vessels at the museum is the *Californian*, the official tall ship of the state of California. This magnificent ship, built in 1984, is a replica of a mid-19th century revenue cutter, a type of ship used by the U.S. government to enforce laws, chase smugglers, and rescue stranded sailors. Unlike some of the older ships at the museum, the *Californian* still sets sail regularly, giving visitors the chance to experience the thrill of sailing on a tall ship. People who climb aboard can learn how to hoist sails, steer the ship, and even help tie the thick ropes that hold the sails in place. The ship's crew, dressed in traditional sailor uniforms, share exciting stories about the life of sailors in the 1800s, explaining how they navigated using only the stars and how they battled fierce storms in the open ocean. For those lucky enough to book a sailing trip on the *Californian*, it's an experience like no other, with the wind filling the sails and the ship gliding smoothly across the water.

The Maritime Museum is also home to something very different from the old sailing ships—a real submarine! The *USS Dolphin* is a deep-diving submarine that was used by the U.S. Navy for research and secret missions. Unlike the other ships, which have wide decks and open spaces, the inside of the *USS Dolphin* is extremely cramped, with narrow passageways, tiny sleeping quarters, and walls covered in buttons, switches, and gauges. Walking through the submarine, visitors get to see how submariners lived and worked underwater for long periods of time. It's fascinating to learn how these vessels could stay submerged for weeks at a time, traveling silently beneath the ocean's surface while carrying out important missions. The *USS Dolphin* holds the record for the deepest dive ever made by a submarine of its kind, and it was used to test new technologies and underwater equipment.

Another must-see ship is the *Berkeley*, a historic steam ferryboat from the late 1800s. This enormous vessel was once used to transport passengers across the San Francisco Bay, and it played an important role in rescuing people during the Great San Francisco Earthquake of 1906. Inside the *Berkeley*, visitors can explore the elegant passenger cabins, complete with beautiful woodwork and stained-glass windows. Unlike the rough conditions on the sailing ships, the ferryboat was designed for comfort, with spacious rooms and plush seating for travelers. The *Berkeley* is also home to many of the museum's exhibits, including displays about shipbuilding, maritime navigation, and life at sea.

The Maritime Museum isn't just about looking at old ships—it's also a place where history comes to life. Throughout the year, the museum hosts special events, reenactments, and hands-on activities that let visitors experience maritime history in exciting ways. Guests can watch sailors demonstrate traditional ship skills, listen to storytellers share tales of daring sea voyages, and even try their hand at knot-tying or signal flag communication. One of the most thrilling events is the museum's pirate-themed adventure, where kids and families can dress up as pirates, go on scavenger hunts, and learn about the real-life buccaneers who once sailed the waters off California's coast.

The museum also offers boat tours and bay cruises, giving visitors a chance to explore San Diego's beautiful waterfront from the deck of a historic ship. Some of these tours even include whale-watching trips, where passengers can see massive gray whales migrating along the California coast. For those interested in the science of sailing, the museum has workshops on how wind, currents, and navigation tools were used to guide ships across the ocean long before modern technology.

A visit to the Maritime Museum of San Diego is like stepping into a giant history book, except instead of just reading about the past, visitors get to experience it firsthand. Whether exploring a tall ship, diving into the world of submarines, or imagining life aboard a ferry from the 1800s, there's something for everyone to enjoy. The ships each have their own unique stories, from grand adventures and daring rescues to scientific discoveries and Hollywood fame. With so much to see and do, the Maritime Museum is a place that keeps visitors coming back for more, eager to uncover new stories and set sail on another journey through history.

Chapter 12: Hiking in Torrey Pines

Torrey Pines State Natural Reserve is one of the most breathtaking places to go hiking in all of San Diego. Nestled along the stunning coastline, this protected area is home to towering cliffs, rare pine trees, and some of the most incredible ocean views in Southern California. Unlike many parks where you just walk through forests or along rivers, Torrey Pines offers a mix of landscapes, from rugged cliffs to sandy beaches, winding trails to sweeping coastal panoramas. Every step along the hiking paths leads to something new and exciting, making it a perfect place for an outdoor adventure. Whether visitors are looking for a relaxing stroll, a challenging climb, or a peaceful spot to watch the sunset, Torrey Pines has it all.

One of the most fascinating things about this reserve is that it is home to the Torrey pine tree, which is one of the rarest pine trees in the world. These trees only grow in two places—here at Torrey Pines and on Santa Rosa Island, which is far off the coast of California. Because they are so rare, they are protected, and hiking through the park gives visitors a chance to see these special trees up close. The trees have twisted, gnarled branches that have been shaped by the coastal winds, making them look like something out of a fairy tale. Some of them have stood for hundreds of years, surviving harsh weather and salty air.

The hiking trails at Torrey Pines range from easy to challenging, so there's something for every type of hiker. One of the most popular trails is the Guy Fleming Trail, which is an easy and short loop that takes visitors to some of the best viewpoints in the reserve. Along this trail, hikers can see wildflowers blooming in the spring, birds soaring above the cliffs, and waves crashing against the rocky shoreline below. This trail is perfect for families or anyone who wants a relaxing walk with stunning scenery. On a clear day, hikers can even spot dolphins or whales swimming in the ocean, making the experience even more magical.

For those looking for a slightly longer hike, the Razor Point Trail is a fantastic choice. This trail winds through dramatic landscapes, with sharp cliffs, deep ravines, and unique rock formations. One of the highlights of this hike is the breathtaking overlook at the end, where hikers can stand on the edge of a cliff and gaze out at the endless blue ocean. The trail is named after the jagged, razor-like formations that have been shaped by wind and rain over thousands of years. Along the way, visitors can see desert-like plants, twisted tree roots, and even small caves carved into the sandstone cliffs.

Another amazing trail is the Beach Trail, which takes hikers all the way down to the sandy shore. This trail is a bit steeper than the others, but the reward at the end is worth every step. As hikers make their way down, they pass through colorful rock layers that reveal the history of the land, with shades of red, orange, and yellow blending together. Once at the beach, visitors can walk along the shore, feel the cool waves washing over their feet, and look up at the towering cliffs they just descended. This is one of the most exciting parts of the reserve because it combines the beauty of both the land and the sea.

Torrey Pines is also a fantastic place for wildlife lovers. Because the reserve is protected, many animals call it home. Hikers often spot rabbits hopping through the bushes, lizards basking in the sun, and hawks soaring overhead. In the early morning or late afternoon, lucky visitors might even see a bobcat sneaking through the underbrush or a coyote trotting along the trail. The park is also a great place for birdwatching, with species like pelicans, ospreys, and even peregrine falcons making their home here. These birds are some of the fastest animals in the world, diving through the sky at incredible speeds to catch their prey.

One of the best times to visit Torrey Pines is during sunset. The entire park glows with golden light, and the ocean reflects brilliant shades of pink, orange, and purple. Watching the sun dip below the horizon from one of the high cliffs is an unforgettable experience. The fresh ocean breeze, the sound of the waves, and the beauty of nature all come together to create a peaceful and magical moment.

Visitors to the reserve should always remember that Torrey Pines is a protected area, which means it's important to stay on the trails and not disturb the plants and wildlife. There are no trash cans inside the reserve, so everyone is expected to take their trash with them and leave no trace. The goal is to keep this beautiful place as natural as possible so future generations can enjoy it just as much as visitors do today.

For those who love both hiking and history, Torrey Pines also has an interesting past. Long before it became a reserve, this land was used by Native American tribes who lived off the resources of the land and sea. They gathered food from the ocean, used plants for medicine, and built homes using natural materials. Later, Spanish explorers and settlers passed through the area, and in the 1800s, scientists recognized how special the Torrey pine trees were and worked to protect them. Thanks to their efforts, the park remains a place of wonder and discovery.

A day spent hiking in Torrey Pines is one of the best ways to connect with nature and experience the beauty of San Diego's coastline. With its rare trees, dramatic cliffs, peaceful trails, and incredible ocean views, it's a place that leaves visitors in awe. Whether walking through the quiet forests, standing at the edge of a towering cliff, or feeling the soft sand beneath their feet, everyone who hikes here comes away with memories that last a lifetime. There's always something new to discover, whether it's a hidden path, a playful dolphin in the water, or a breathtaking sunset that fills the sky with color. No matter how many times someone visits, Torrey Pines never stops being a place of adventure, beauty, and wonder.

Chapter 13: Science Fun at Fleet Center

The Fleet Science Center in San Diego is one of the most exciting places for anyone who loves science, technology, and hands-on exploration. Located in the heart of Balboa Park, this amazing science center is packed with interactive exhibits, fun experiments, and mind-blowing demonstrations that make learning exciting for visitors of all ages. Unlike a regular museum where you just look at things, the Fleet Center encourages visitors to touch, build, play, and experiment with science in ways that make it come alive. From outer space to deep-sea exploration, from human biology to high-tech inventions, there is something fascinating to discover around every corner.

One of the first things visitors notice when they step into the Fleet Science Center is the giant dome theater, which is one of the most impressive parts of the museum. This is no ordinary movie screen—it's a huge, curved IMAX dome that surrounds the audience, making them feel like they are inside the film itself. The theater shows incredible science documentaries that take viewers on amazing journeys, like diving deep into the ocean, traveling through the solar system, or even shrinking down to explore the human body from the inside. The combination of giant visuals and powerful sound makes every film an unforgettable experience. It's almost like being on a real adventure without ever leaving your seat.

After watching a thrilling show in the theater, visitors can explore the many exhibits throughout the museum. One of the most exciting areas is the "Block Busters" exhibit, which is all about engineering and building. Here, kids and adults alike can construct towers, bridges, and other structures using blocks, magnets, and other materials. It's a great way to learn about physics, balance, and design while having tons of fun. Visitors can even test their creations by putting them on platforms that shake to simulate earthquakes, helping them understand how engineers design buildings to withstand natural disasters.

Another must-visit area is the "Kid City" exhibit, which is perfect for younger visitors. This miniature city allows kids to play and learn about science at the same time. There are stations where they can experiment with air pressure, water flow, and gears, helping them understand important scientific concepts in a fun and engaging way. There's even a child-sized grocery store where kids can scan items and learn about how different machines work in everyday life.

For those interested in space and astronomy, the "Space Gallery" is a dream come true. This section of the museum is all about the wonders of the universe, from planets and stars to black holes and galaxies. Visitors can learn what it feels like to walk on the Moon by stepping onto a special simulator, or they can test their knowledge of the solar system with interactive displays that explain how planets orbit the Sun. One of the coolest features in this exhibit is a real-life Mars rover model, just like the ones NASA has sent to explore the Red Planet. Visitors can control the rover and try navigating it over rocky terrain, just like real scientists do when they explore other planets.

If robots and high-tech inventions sound exciting, then the "Innovation Lab" is the perfect place to visit. This section of the museum is filled with futuristic technology, from robotic arms to artificial intelligence. Visitors can try coding a robot to follow specific commands, or they can experiment with 3D printing to see how objects are created layer by layer. There are also hands-on challenges where visitors must use creativity and problem-solving skills to complete engineering tasks, like building a bridge that can hold weight or designing a flying contraption.

One of the most mind-blowing exhibits at the Fleet Science Center is the "Illusions and Perceptions" gallery. This section is all about tricking the brain and discovering how our senses can sometimes deceive us. There are spinning tunnels that make visitors feel like they are losing their balance, mirrors that create optical illusions, and puzzles that challenge the way people see colors, patterns, and movement. It's a great way to learn about how the human brain processes information and why we sometimes see things differently than they really are.

For those fascinated by the human body, the "You and Your Body" exhibit is a fantastic place to explore. Visitors can test their reflexes, measure their heart rate, and even see how their muscles and bones work together to help them move. One of the most popular parts of this exhibit is the giant walk-through heart, where visitors can step inside and see how blood flows through different chambers. There are also interactive displays that show what happens inside the body when we exercise, sleep, or eat different types of food.

In addition to all these exciting exhibits, the Fleet Science Center also hosts live science demonstrations throughout the day. These shows feature incredible experiments, like making giant bubbles, launching rockets, or even creating explosions using chemistry. The presenters explain the science behind each experiment in a fun and entertaining way, making it easy to understand while keeping the audience amazed.

For visitors who love solving mysteries, the "Puzzle Lab" is a fantastic place to test problem-solving skills. This exhibit is filled with brain teasers, logic games, and hands-on challenges that encourage visitors to think creatively and work as a team. There are mazes to navigate, locks to open, and riddles to solve, making it one of the most interactive areas in the museum.

Another fascinating feature of the Fleet Science Center is its focus on environmental science and sustainability. The "Eco Explorers" exhibit teaches visitors about how humans can help protect the planet by using renewable energy, recycling, and conserving water. There are interactive stations where visitors can experiment with solar panels, wind turbines, and other green technologies to see how they work. This exhibit is a great way to learn about how science can be used to create a healthier and more sustainable world.

The fun at the Fleet Science Center doesn't end inside the building—there are also outdoor exhibits and activities to explore. The museum has a science-themed playground where kids can climb, slide, and discover science in action. There's even a giant whisper dish, where people can stand on opposite sides of a large dish and whisper to each other, hearing the sound travel clearly across a long distance.

For those who want to take the science fun home with them, the Fleet Science Center has an amazing gift shop filled with educational toys, science kits, and books. Visitors can find everything from build-your-own robot kits to glow-in-the-dark stars for their ceiling. It's the perfect place to find a souvenir that keeps the excitement of science going long after leaving the museum.

The Fleet Science Center is also known for hosting special events, including science camps, workshops, and even sleepovers where visitors can spend the night inside the museum. These events give kids and families the chance to dive even deeper into science topics and participate in unique activities that aren't available during regular museum hours.

A visit to the Fleet Science Center is an unforgettable experience that sparks curiosity, creativity, and a love for learning. Whether exploring the wonders of space, building and testing inventions, solving mind-bending puzzles, or watching explosive science demonstrations, there is always something new and exciting to discover. With so many interactive exhibits and hands-on activities, the Fleet Science Center proves that science isn't just something you read about in books—it's something you can see, touch, and experience in the most thrilling ways possible. No matter how many times someone visits, there's always a new experiment to try, a new mystery to solve, and a new adventure waiting to be explored.

Chapter 14: Shopping in Seaport Village

Seaport Village is one of the most magical places in San Diego, where shopping, entertainment, and stunning waterfront views all come together in a beautiful setting. Located right next to the sparkling San Diego Bay, this charming shopping area feels like a little coastal town of its own, with winding walkways, colorful buildings, and a relaxing atmosphere that makes every visit feel like a vacation. Unlike a giant mall with rows of ordinary stores, Seaport Village is designed to feel cozy and unique, with small boutique shops, local artisans, and one-of-a-kind treasures waiting to be discovered at every turn.

Walking into Seaport Village feels like stepping into a different world, where the salty sea breeze fills the air and palm trees sway gently under the California sun. The pathways are lined with more than 50 unique stores, each offering something special that you won't find anywhere else. Some shops sell beautiful handmade jewelry, while others are packed with souvenirs, clothing, artwork, and creative gifts that capture the spirit of San Diego. Many of the stores are tucked inside quaint wooden cottages and Spanish-style buildings, giving the village a warm and inviting feel.

One of the best parts of shopping at Seaport Village is that it's not just about buying things—it's about exploring and experiencing something new. There's a shop for every kind of interest, whether you love books, music, fashion, or fun collectibles. For those who love creative and artistic items, Seaport Village is home to several specialty shops that sell handmade crafts, paintings, and sculptures made by local artists. Some stores even let visitors watch artists at work, creating stunning pieces right in front of their eyes. It's a wonderful way to see creativity in action and take home something truly unique.

For book lovers, there are cozy little bookstores filled with fascinating reads about everything from San Diego's history to adventures around the world. These shops often carry books signed by local authors, making them extra special. If you're someone who enjoys music, there are stores that sell old records, unique instruments, and fun musical gifts. Stepping inside, you might hear the sounds of classic jazz, rock, or traditional folk music playing in the background, adding to the magical experience.

For visitors who love fashion, Seaport Village has clothing boutiques filled with stylish outfits, beachwear, and accessories that fit the laid-back San Diego lifestyle. There are shops with breezy summer dresses, cool T-shirts with fun San Diego designs, and comfortable sandals perfect for walking along the waterfront. Some stores specialize in hats, sunglasses, and other accessories that are great for sunny days. There's even a shop that sells colorful socks with silly patterns, making it a fun stop for anyone who enjoys quirky fashion.

One of the most exciting parts of shopping in Seaport Village is the toy and novelty stores that are filled with fun surprises. There are shops packed with puzzles, games, and stuffed animals, making them a perfect stop for kids and kids-at-heart. Some stores carry old-fashioned toys that parents and grandparents might remember from their childhood, creating a fun mix of nostalgia and new discoveries. There are also magic shops where visitors can learn cool tricks and buy their own magician's kit to impress their friends. Some of these stores even have magicians performing live demonstrations, showing off amazing card tricks and illusions.

For those who love sweet treats and delicious snacks, Seaport Village is a paradise of tasty discoveries. There are candy shops filled with chocolates, jelly beans, caramel apples, and saltwater taffy in dozens of flavors. Some stores sell handmade fudge, letting visitors watch as chocolatiers pour and shape the delicious treats right in front of them. If you're a fan of gourmet popcorn, there are shops with bags of freshly popped kernels in flavors like cheese, caramel, and even spicy chili. One of the most popular snack stops in Seaport Village is the old-fashioned ice cream parlor, where visitors can choose from a huge variety of flavors, from classic vanilla and chocolate to unique creations like coconut pineapple and mint chip. Eating a scoop of ice cream while strolling along the waterfront is one of the best ways to enjoy the village.

Another highlight of shopping at Seaport Village is the beautiful home décor stores that sell beach-themed decorations, cozy candles, and handcrafted furniture. These shops are perfect for anyone who wants to bring a little bit of the coastal charm of San Diego into their own home. Some stores sell hand-painted seashells, while others have driftwood sculptures and ocean-inspired artwork. There are also shops that sell colorful Mexican pottery and decorative tiles, perfect for adding a splash of culture and creativity to any space.

Seaport Village is also home to several specialty gift shops that sell fun and unusual souvenirs. Some stores have entire sections dedicated to pirates, with treasure maps, model ships, and toy swords that make visitors feel like they've stepped onto a pirate's island. Others sell funny T-shirts and mugs with silly San Diego jokes and slogans. There are even shops dedicated to pets, where visitors can buy adorable outfits, toys, and treats for their furry friends.

One of the most famous and beloved shops in Seaport Village is the kite store, which has been a favorite for generations. This store is packed with colorful kites of all shapes and sizes, from simple diamond kites to massive, elaborate ones shaped like dragons, butterflies, and even spaceships. On windy days, visitors can see kites soaring high above the waterfront, creating a beautiful and joyful scene. The shop owners are always happy to give advice on how to fly a kite, making it a fun and interactive experience for families and visitors of all ages.

Shopping in Seaport Village isn't just about the stores—it's also about the experience of being in such a lively and beautiful place. Musicians often perform along the pathways, playing everything from soft acoustic guitar melodies to energetic mariachi tunes. There are street performers who juggle, do magic tricks, and even create balloon animals for kids. The village also has lovely little gardens and fountains where visitors can sit and relax while enjoying the peaceful sounds of the bay.

After a long day of shopping, visitors can take a break at one of the many waterfront restaurants and cafés in Seaport Village. Some places serve fresh seafood, like fish tacos and shrimp platters, while others offer delicious burgers, sandwiches, and pizzas. There are also charming little coffee shops where visitors can sip a warm drink while watching sailboats glide across the bay. Some restaurants have outdoor seating with breathtaking views of the water, making them the perfect place to enjoy a meal while soaking in the beauty of San Diego.

As the sun starts to set, Seaport Village takes on an even more magical atmosphere. The twinkling lights of the shops and restaurants reflect off the water, creating a picture-perfect scene. Visitors can take a relaxing stroll along the waterfront, watch the boats come in, or even hop on a horse-drawn carriage for a charming ride around the village. With the cool ocean breeze and the sounds of laughter and music filling the air, it's easy to see why Seaport Village is one of the most beloved places in San Diego.

Shopping at Seaport Village is more than just a trip to the store—it's an adventure filled with discoveries, delicious treats, and unforgettable moments. Whether browsing for unique souvenirs, watching street performers, flying a kite, or enjoying a scoop of ice cream by the bay, every visit to this wonderful seaside village is a special experience. No matter how many times you visit, there's always something new to explore, making it a must-see destination for anyone who wants to experience the heart and soul of San Diego.

Chapter 15: Delicious Mexican Food

San Diego is one of the best places in the United States to enjoy delicious Mexican food. Because the city is right next to the Mexican border, the flavors and traditions of Mexico are woven into everyday life, especially when it comes to food. From tiny taco stands to fancy restaurants, San Diego is bursting with incredible dishes that are packed with bold, fresh, and zesty flavors. Whether it's tacos, burritos, enchiladas, tamales, or sizzling fajitas, there's always something mouthwatering to try.

One of the most famous Mexican dishes in San Diego is the taco. A taco might seem simple, but the variety of tacos in San Diego is endless. Some people like soft corn tortillas filled with slow-cooked beef or spicy pork, while others prefer crispy shells packed with seasoned chicken or grilled vegetables. Then there are fish tacos, a San Diego specialty, which feature crispy or grilled fish topped with crunchy cabbage, creamy sauce, and a squeeze of fresh lime. Some tacos are topped with fresh pico de gallo, which is a mix of chopped tomatoes, onions, cilantro, and lime juice that adds a burst of freshness to every bite. Others come with spicy salsa, rich guacamole, or melted cheese for an extra layer of deliciousness.

Another Mexican dish that San Diego is known for is the burrito. A burrito is a large, soft flour tortilla stuffed with all kinds of tasty ingredients. Some burritos are filled with beans, rice, and cheese, while others include grilled steak, shredded chicken, or spicy chorizo sausage. One of the most famous types of burritos in San Diego is the California burrito, which is stuffed with carne asada (grilled steak), French fries, cheese, sour cream, and guacamole. This combination might sound unusual at first, but once you take a bite, the mix of flavors and textures is absolutely incredible. Some burritos are smothered in red or green sauce and topped with melted cheese, turning them into a dish called a "wet burrito," which is eaten with a fork and knife.

Tamales are another classic Mexican dish that people in San Diego love. A tamale is made by spreading a layer of soft corn dough, called masa, onto a corn husk and filling it with meat, cheese, or even sweet ingredients like cinnamon and raisins. The tamale is then wrapped up and steamed until it becomes soft and flavorful. When it's ready to eat, the husk is peeled away, revealing a warm, fluffy tamale inside. Many families in San Diego enjoy tamales during special holidays, like Christmas and Día de los Muertos, but they are also available at Mexican restaurants and markets all year round.

If you love cheesy, saucy dishes, enchiladas are a must-try. Enchiladas are corn tortillas rolled up with meat, cheese, or beans inside, then covered in a rich and flavorful sauce. There are different types of enchilada sauces, including red sauce made from tomatoes and chilies, green sauce made from tangy tomatillos, and mole sauce, which is a thick, dark sauce made from chocolate, spices, and chilies. The enchiladas are then baked with melted cheese on top, creating a warm and comforting dish that is full of flavor.

San Diego is also famous for its sizzling fajitas. Fajitas are made with strips of grilled meat, such as steak or chicken, cooked with bell peppers and onions. When they are served at a restaurant, they often come on a hot, steaming plate that sizzles as it arrives at the table. Fajitas are usually eaten with soft tortillas, so you can build your own delicious wrap with the sizzling meat, fresh toppings, and tasty sauces.

For those who love spicy and flavorful soups, pozole is a fantastic dish to try. Pozole is a traditional Mexican soup made with hominy, which is a type of large, soft corn, along with tender pieces of pork or chicken. The soup is simmered with spices and chilies, giving it a deep, rich flavor. When served, pozole comes with toppings like shredded cabbage, radishes, lime, and crispy tortilla strips, which add crunch and freshness to every spoonful.

Another comforting dish that is popular in San Diego is chiles rellenos. A chile relleno is a large, mild green chili pepper stuffed with cheese, dipped in a light batter, and fried until golden and crispy. The outside is slightly crunchy, while the inside is warm and gooey from the melted cheese. Chiles rellenos are often served with rice, beans, and a tasty tomato sauce that soaks into the crispy batter, making each bite even more delicious.

Mexican food in San Diego isn't just about full meals—it's also about tasty snacks and street food. One of the most popular street snacks is elote, or Mexican street corn. Elote is grilled corn on the cob that is slathered with mayonnaise, sprinkled with crumbled cheese, dusted with chili powder, and finished with a squeeze of fresh lime juice. The combination of smoky, creamy, spicy, and tangy flavors makes this a favorite treat at food trucks and street markets.

Churros are another must-try Mexican snack that is especially loved by those with a sweet tooth. Churros are long, crispy pastries made from fried dough, coated in cinnamon sugar, and often served with a side of warm chocolate sauce for dipping. Some churros are even stuffed with sweet fillings like caramel or chocolate, making them extra irresistible.

One of the best things about Mexican food in San Diego is the fresh ingredients that make every dish taste amazing. Many restaurants use handmade tortillas, freshly chopped salsas, and high-quality meats and vegetables to create their dishes. Guacamole, for example, is always made fresh with ripe avocados, lime juice, tomatoes, and cilantro, giving it a creamy and refreshing flavor that pairs perfectly with tacos, burritos, or just a basket of crispy tortilla chips.

San Diego is home to many family-owned Mexican restaurants, where recipes have been passed down for generations. Some of these places have been serving delicious Mexican food for decades, with secret spice blends and cooking techniques that make their dishes extra special. There are also modern Mexican restaurants that put a creative twist on traditional dishes, offering new and exciting flavors while still honoring the rich history of Mexican cuisine.

For those who want to experience the most authentic flavors, visiting a Mexican market or food festival in San Diego is a great way to explore even more delicious options. At these markets, visitors can find handmade tamales, fresh tortillas being pressed and cooked right in front of them, and giant pots of simmering stews that fill the air with incredible aromas. Food festivals often feature live music, dancing, and cooking demonstrations, making them a fun and tasty way to learn more about Mexican culture and cuisine.

No matter what type of Mexican food you try in San Diego, one thing is certain—every dish is full of bold flavors, vibrant colors, and a rich cultural history that makes each bite special. Whether you're enjoying tacos by the beach, a burrito from a food truck, or a warm bowl of pozole on a cool evening, the experience of eating Mexican food in San Diego is always an adventure. With so many incredible dishes to try, it's no wonder that people from all over come to this city to experience some of the best Mexican food in the world.

Chapter 16: Sports and Stadiums

San Diego is a city that loves sports, and there are plenty of exciting games, teams, and stadiums that bring people together to cheer for their favorite athletes. Whether it's baseball, football, soccer, or even surfing competitions, San Diego offers something for every sports fan. The city's warm weather and beautiful scenery make it the perfect place for outdoor sports, and its modern stadiums give fans a great place to watch all the action. From thrilling professional games to local tournaments and beachside sports, there's never a shortage of ways to enjoy athletic events in this energetic city.

One of the most famous sports teams in San Diego is the San Diego Padres, the city's professional baseball team. The Padres play at Petco Park, a massive stadium located in downtown San Diego. This ballpark is not just a place to watch baseball—it's an experience. The stadium has stunning views of the San Diego skyline, delicious food options, and even a park area where families can sit on the grass and watch the game. Fans of the Padres fill the stadium wearing the team's signature colors—brown and gold—while cheering loudly when their team hits a home run. Baseball season lasts from spring to fall, and attending a Padres game is a tradition for many San Diegans. Some games even end with a spectacular fireworks show, making the experience even more exciting.

Another important sports team in San Diego is the San Diego Wave FC, the city's professional women's soccer team. They play at Snapdragon Stadium, which is one of the newest sports venues in the city. This team is part of the National Women's Soccer League (NWSL) and has some of the best female soccer players in the country. When the Wave plays, the stadium fills with fans waving blue and white flags, chanting team songs, and celebrating every goal with huge cheers. San Diego has always been a city that loves soccer, and having a professional women's team has brought even more excitement to the sport.

In addition to the Wave, another soccer team that plays in San Diego is the San Diego Loyal SC, a men's team that competes in the United Soccer League (USL). Soccer fans in San Diego are passionate about their teams, and games often have a lively atmosphere with loud drumbeats, colorful banners, and dedicated fans who never stop cheering. Because soccer is such a popular sport in San Diego, many kids and adults enjoy playing the game themselves, whether in organized leagues or casual matches at parks and beaches.

Football has also played a big role in San Diego's sports history. For many years, the city was home to the San Diego Chargers, an NFL team that played at Qualcomm Stadium (now the site of Snapdragon Stadium). Although the team moved to Los Angeles, many San Diegans are still passionate football fans. College football is also popular, with the San Diego State Aztecs being the main team representing the city. Their games are held at Snapdragon Stadium, and fans fill the stands wearing red and black to support their team. The energy at a college football game is electrifying, with marching bands playing music, cheerleaders leading chants, and fans jumping to their feet with every big play.

Basketball fans in San Diego also have plenty to enjoy. While the city doesn't have an NBA team, it does have the San Diego State Aztecs men's basketball team, which has been highly successful in college basketball. They play their home games at Viejas Arena, an indoor stadium on the campus of San Diego State University. When the Aztecs are doing well, their games can be packed with fans who love the fast-paced excitement of basketball. Some of the best college basketball tournaments, such as the NCAA March Madness games, have also been held in San Diego, bringing in fans from all over the country.

Beyond traditional sports like baseball, soccer, football, and basketball, San Diego is also famous for its outdoor and water sports.

Because of its incredible coastline, the city hosts some of the best surfing competitions in the world. Professional surfers come to San Diego to compete in events where they ride giant waves and show off their impressive skills. The U.S. Open of Surfing, one of the most well-known surfing events, often has competitors from all over the world. Even if you're not competing, San Diego's beaches are a great place to watch surfers catch waves or try surfing yourself.

Another popular outdoor sport in San Diego is golf. The city is home to some of the most beautiful golf courses in the country, including the famous Torrey Pines Golf Course. This course, located on cliffs overlooking the Pacific Ocean, hosts the PGA Tour's Farmers Insurance Open every year. Professional golfers come to San Diego to play on this challenging and scenic course, and golf fans love watching the tournament to see some of the best players in the world compete. There are also many other golf courses throughout the city where beginners and experts alike can enjoy the game.

For those who enjoy extreme sports, San Diego has plenty of options as well. Skateboarding is extremely popular in the city, with many skate parks available for people to practice their tricks. The sport has deep roots in San Diego, as many of the world's best skateboarders grew up here and helped make skateboarding famous. There are also BMX biking competitions, where athletes perform amazing stunts on bikes, and rock climbing gyms where people can test their strength and skill.

San Diego is also home to the Holiday Bowl, an annual college football game that takes place at Petco Park. This game brings in teams from different parts of the country to compete in front of thousands of fans. It's one of the biggest football events in the city and includes a huge parade with marching bands, decorated floats, and lots of school spirit. Many people in San Diego look forward to the Holiday Bowl every year as a way to celebrate both sports and the holiday season.

With so many teams, stadiums, and exciting events, San Diego is a paradise for sports fans. Whether you enjoy cheering for the Padres at Petco Park, watching world-class surfers ride the waves, playing soccer at a local park, or attending a big college football game, there is always something happening in this lively city. The combination of professional teams, incredible stadiums, and a love for outdoor activities makes San Diego one of the best places in the country for sports lovers. Whether you're watching or playing, sports are a big part of life in this amazing city.

Chapter 17: Festivals and Parades

San Diego is a city full of life, energy, and excitement, and one of the best ways to experience its vibrant culture is through its amazing festivals and parades. Throughout the year, the city comes alive with celebrations that showcase music, art, food, history, and traditions from around the world. Whether it's a colorful parade marching through the streets, a lively music festival on the beach, or a cultural event filled with delicious food and traditional performances, there's always something exciting happening in San Diego. These events bring people together, creating unforgettable memories for both locals and visitors. No matter what time of year you visit, there's a good chance you'll get to experience one of San Diego's incredible festivals or parades.

One of the biggest and most famous festivals in San Diego is Comic-Con International. Every summer, thousands of people from all over the world come to the San Diego Convention Center to celebrate comic books, movies, TV shows, video games, and pop culture. Fans dress up as their favorite characters in elaborate costumes, and the streets of downtown San Diego turn into a giant party. At Comic-Con, you can meet famous actors, watch exciting previews of upcoming movies, see incredible artwork, and buy all kinds of cool collectibles. Even if you don't have a ticket to the convention, the entire city gets involved, with restaurants, hotels, and public spaces decorating for the occasion. It's one of the most exciting times to be in San Diego, especially if you love superheroes, sci-fi, and fantasy.

Another huge event in San Diego is the annual Holiday Bowl Parade, which takes place every December. This is the largest balloon parade in the country, featuring massive, colorful helium balloons floating above the streets, marching bands playing festive tunes, and beautifully decorated floats rolling past cheering crowds. The parade is part of the Holiday Bowl, a college football game that brings in teams from across the country. Families gather along the streets to watch the parade, enjoying the festive atmosphere filled with holiday cheer. The event is a wonderful way to celebrate the season, and the excitement continues with fireworks, performances, and, of course, the big football game.

For those who love history and culture, San Diego's Old Town Dia de los Muertos celebration is a must-see. Dia de los Muertos, or Day of the Dead, is a Mexican tradition that honors loved ones who have passed away. In Old Town, the heart of San Diego's Mexican heritage, the celebration is filled with colorful altars, marigold flowers, and beautiful skeleton face paintings. Families create ofrendas (offerings) decorated with candles, food, and photographs to remember their ancestors. The event includes traditional music, dancing, storytelling, and delicious Mexican food like pan de muerto, a special sweet bread. People of all ages come to experience this rich cultural tradition, learning about its meaning while enjoying the lively festivities.

San Diego is also home to the famous Lunar New Year Festival, which celebrates the Chinese New Year with dragon dances, fireworks, martial arts performances, and traditional Asian cuisine. The festival is held in different parts of the city, including the San Diego Zoo, Balboa Park, and the Convoy District, where there is a large Asian community. Visitors can watch lion dancers move to the rhythm of beating drums, enjoy delicious dumplings and noodles, and take part in fun activities like calligraphy and lantern-making. It's a special time to welcome good luck, prosperity, and happiness for the new year.

For those who love music and dancing, the San Diego Latino Film Festival and the San Diego Salsa Bachata Festival are two incredible events that highlight Latin American culture. The film festival showcases movies from Latin American filmmakers, offering a glimpse into different cultures, traditions, and stories from around the world. Meanwhile, the Salsa Bachata Festival is a lively event where people can dance to energetic Latin beats, take lessons from professional dancers, and enjoy live performances by talented musicians. Whether you're an expert dancer or just love listening to music, these festivals bring a fun and festive atmosphere to the city.

San Diego's Pride Parade and Festival is one of the largest and most colorful events of the year, celebrating love, diversity, and equality. The parade features vibrant floats, creative costumes, and thousands of people marching in support of LGBTQ+ rights. The festival that follows includes live music, delicious food, and exciting performances. Families, friends, and visitors from all over come together to celebrate love and acceptance in a joyful and welcoming environment.

If you love food, then you won't want to miss the San Diego Bay Wine & Food Festival. This event is a paradise for food lovers, featuring some of the best chefs, restaurants, and wineries in the region. Visitors can sample gourmet dishes, try different types of wine, and watch live cooking demonstrations by top chefs. The festival takes place along the beautiful waterfront, making it a perfect place to enjoy delicious food while admiring stunning ocean views. There are also taco festivals, seafood festivals, and even a special event dedicated to chocolate, where visitors can try all kinds of sweet treats.

For a mix of history and adventure, Fleet Week San Diego is a spectacular event that honors the U.S. Navy, Marine Corps, and Coast Guard. The celebration includes ship tours, air shows featuring military jets, and parades honoring service members. One of the highlights is watching the Navy SEALs perform demonstrations in the water, showing their incredible skills and bravery. Visitors can step aboard massive naval ships, meet military personnel, and even watch paratroopers skydiving into the harbor. It's a thrilling experience that gives people a chance to appreciate the men and women who serve in the armed forces.

San Diego is also known for its incredible Fourth of July celebrations, with breathtaking fireworks lighting up the night sky over the bay. The biggest fireworks show is the Big Bay Boom, where multiple locations around the waterfront launch fireworks at the same time, creating a spectacular display of lights and colors. People gather at beaches, parks, and even boats to watch the show, while enjoying barbecues, picnics, and fun activities throughout the day. The energy and excitement of Independence Day make it one of the most fun and patriotic celebrations in the city.

Another fascinating festival is the Cabrillo Festival, which celebrates the discovery of California by Spanish explorer Juan Rodriguez Cabrillo. This historical event takes place at Cabrillo National Monument and includes reenactments, storytelling, and performances that bring the past to life. Visitors can watch actors dressed as 16th-century explorers, learn about the early days of California, and take part in fun activities like shipbuilding demonstrations and guided nature walks. It's a great way to experience history while enjoying the stunning views of the Pacific Ocean.

With so many festivals and parades happening year-round, San Diego is a city that never stops celebrating. Whether it's a massive event like Comic-Con, a cultural celebration like Dia de los Muertos, or a lively music festival by the beach, there's always something fun and exciting to experience. These festivals bring people together, allowing them to enjoy music, food, art, and traditions from around the world. Whether you love sports, music, history, or food, San Diego's festivals and parades offer endless opportunities for adventure, discovery, and fun.

Chapter 18: Ghost Stories of Old San Diego

San Diego may be famous for its sunny beaches, exciting attractions, and beautiful weather, but did you know that it also has a spooky side? The city is filled with history, and with history come ghost stories that have been passed down for generations. From haunted houses to eerie hotels and old cemeteries, San Diego has its fair share of mysterious places where strange things are said to happen. Whether you believe in ghosts or not, the chilling tales of Old San Diego's past are sure to send shivers down your spine. Some of these stories come from the time when Spanish explorers first arrived, while others date back to the Wild West days, when gunfights, outlaws, and untimely deaths were a part of life. If you ever visit San Diego, you might just find yourself in a place where history and the supernatural collide.

One of the most famous haunted locations in San Diego is the Whaley House, which is often called one of the most haunted houses in America. This old mansion, located in Old Town San Diego, has a long and eerie history. It was built in 1857 by Thomas Whaley, a wealthy businessman, but even before the house was built, the land already had a dark past. It was once the site of public executions, where criminals were hanged in front of large crowds. One of the most famous ghosts believed to haunt the Whaley House is that of Yankee Jim Robinson, a man who was sentenced to death and hanged right where the house now stands. Visitors have reported hearing heavy footsteps echoing through the halls, even when no one is there. Some people claim to have seen a tall, shadowy figure wandering through the rooms, while others feel an icy chill in the air, even on the warmest days.

The Whaley family themselves also had a history of tragedy, which may explain why their spirits are said to linger in the house. Thomas Whaley's daughter, Violet, suffered from depression after a failed marriage and tragically took her own life in the house. Her ghost is said to be seen standing near the staircase, dressed in a long gown, her expression sorrowful. Other members of the Whaley family are also believed to haunt the home, with guests reporting seeing a woman in a flowing dress, the laughter of a child, and even the scent of old-fashioned perfume filling the air. Today, the Whaley House is a museum, and visitors from all over the world come to see if they can catch a glimpse of one of its many ghosts.

Another eerie location in San Diego is the Hotel del Coronado, a stunning beachfront hotel with a dark secret. The hotel, built in 1888, has long been known for its luxurious beauty and celebrity guests, but it is also famous for being haunted by the spirit of a woman named Kate Morgan. Kate checked into the hotel in 1892, but she was found dead on the steps leading down to the beach just a few days later. Her death was ruled a suicide, but many people believe there was more to the story. Some say she was waiting for a lover who never arrived, while others think there may have been foul play involved.

Kate's ghost is said to still wander the halls of the Hotel del Coronado. Guests who stay in the room she occupied have reported flickering lights, strange noises, and sudden drops in temperature. Some have even claimed to see the ghostly figure of a woman in a black dress drifting through the halls or standing near the windows, gazing out at the ocean as if waiting for someone who will never come. The hotel embraces its spooky reputation, and many visitors come specifically to learn about the mysterious legend of Kate Morgan.

If you're looking for a truly eerie experience, you might want to visit El Campo Santo Cemetery, one of the oldest burial grounds in San Diego. This small cemetery, located in Old Town, dates back to 1849 and is the final resting place of many early settlers, including criminals, pioneers, and Native Americans. Over the years, parts of the cemetery were paved over to make room for roads and buildings, meaning that some of the graves are now hidden beneath modern-day streets. Many people believe this has disturbed the spirits, leading to ghostly encounters in the area.

Visitors have reported seeing shadowy figures moving through the cemetery at night, and some say they have felt invisible hands pulling on their clothes or tapping them on the shoulder. Car alarms have been known to go off by themselves when parked near the cemetery, and streetlights sometimes flicker on and off for no reason. One of the most famous ghostly sightings is that of a man dressed in 19th-century clothing who appears near the graves and then vanishes without a trace.

San Diego's haunted history doesn't stop there. The Star of India, an old sailing ship docked in San Diego's harbor, is another place where ghostly activity has been reported. This ship, which was built in 1863, has a long history of tragic events. Many sailors and passengers died aboard the ship, and some of their spirits are said to remain. Crew members and visitors have reported hearing ghostly whispers, seeing figures in old-fashioned sailor uniforms, and feeling an eerie presence on board. Some say they have seen the spirit of a young stowaway who fell from the rigging and died on the deck. His presence is often felt in the lower parts of the ship, where people experience sudden cold spots and hear the sound of footsteps when no one is there.

Another famously haunted location is the Horton Grand Hotel in downtown San Diego. This historic hotel is said to be haunted by the ghost of Roger Whittaker, a gambler who was shot and killed in one of the rooms. Guests staying in that room have reported hearing mysterious noises, doors opening and closing on their own, and even seeing ghostly figures in the mirror. Some visitors have also claimed to feel an unseen force tugging at their blankets while they sleep.

San Diego's ghostly legends go beyond just buildings and cemeteries. Even some of the city's natural areas have spooky tales. The Presidio Park, which sits on a hill overlooking Old Town, is said to be haunted by the spirits of Spanish soldiers and Native Americans who once lived there. At night, visitors have reported seeing glowing figures, hearing footsteps in the dark, and feeling an unexplained sense of unease.

With so many ghostly stories tied to its past, San Diego is truly a city where history and the supernatural come together. Whether it's the lingering spirits of the Whaley House, the mysterious presence of Kate Morgan at the Hotel del Coronado, the restless ghosts of El Campo Santo Cemetery, or the haunted halls of old hotels and ships, the city is full of eerie legends waiting to be explored. Some people visit these places hoping to experience a ghostly encounter for themselves, while others prefer to simply hear the stories and imagine the mysteries of the past. Whether you believe in ghosts or not, one thing is certain—San Diego's haunted history is filled with fascinating tales that continue to capture the imagination of those who dare to listen.

Chapter 19: Music and Art Scenes

San Diego is not only known for its sunny beaches and exciting attractions but also for its incredible music and art scenes. The city is bursting with creativity, from live concerts and street performances to museums and colorful murals decorating the walls of different neighborhoods. Whether you love music, painting, dancing, or theater, there's something for everyone in San Diego's artistic world. Musicians and artists from all over come to this city to share their talent, and you can find live music playing somewhere almost every night. The art scene is just as vibrant, with galleries, exhibitions, and outdoor art displays making San Diego a place full of imagination and inspiration. Whether you visit a famous venue, walk through an artsy neighborhood, or stumble upon a talented street musician, you'll quickly see that this city has a deep love for music and art.

One of the best places to experience San Diego's artistic culture is Balboa Park. This massive park isn't just home to gardens and museums—it's also a hub for creativity. The park has numerous art museums, including the San Diego Museum of Art, where you can see paintings, sculptures, and artifacts from all around the world. It's a great place to admire works by famous artists and learn about different styles of art. The park also has the Spanish Village Art Center, a collection of little colorful cottages where local artists create and sell their work. You can watch painters, potters, and jewelry makers as they turn their ideas into beautiful pieces. It's an amazing place to find unique souvenirs or even try your hand at making art yourself. Walking through the park, you might also come across musicians playing guitars, violinists filling the air with lovely melodies, and even street performers putting on entertaining shows.

San Diego is home to many music venues, from small cozy cafes where local musicians perform to large concert halls where world-famous bands play. One of the most iconic music spots in the city is the House of Blues. This lively venue hosts concerts featuring rock, jazz, blues, and pop artists. Whether you enjoy listening to classic rock songs or discovering new bands, the House of Blues is a great place to experience live music. Another fantastic venue is the Rady Shell at Jacobs Park, an outdoor concert space with a breathtaking view of the San Diego Bay. Imagine listening to a live orchestra or a band while feeling the ocean breeze—it's a magical experience! The Casbah is another famous venue, known for its intimate setting where you can get up close to the stage and feel the energy of the music. Many well-known musicians started their careers performing at the Casbah, so you never know when you might be watching the next big star in action.

For those who love musicals and plays, San Diego has a fantastic theater scene. The Old Globe Theatre, located in Balboa Park, is one of the most famous theaters in the city. It was inspired by the original Globe Theatre in London, where Shakespeare's plays were performed centuries ago. Here, you can watch amazing productions of classic plays, modern dramas, and even brand-new shows before they make their way to Broadway. The La Jolla Playhouse is another fantastic theater where incredible performances take place. Many Broadway musicals have actually started right here in San Diego before becoming world-famous, so watching a show in this theater is like getting a sneak peek at something extraordinary before the rest of the world sees it.

San Diego's neighborhoods are also filled with creativity, and one of the best places to experience this is in North Park. This trendy neighborhood is known for its street art, live music, and independent galleries. Walking through North Park, you'll see giant murals painted on buildings, colorful graffiti that tells a story, and sculptures decorating the streets. The neighborhood is also full of coffee shops and small music venues where talented musicians perform. Every year, North Park hosts an arts festival where painters, sculptors, photographers, and musicians come together to showcase their work.

It's a lively event where you can meet artists, watch live performances, and even take part in art activities yourself.

Another must-visit neighborhood for art lovers is Barrio Logan. This area is home to Chicano Park, one of the most famous outdoor art spaces in San Diego. The park is filled with massive murals painted on the pillars of a highway bridge, each one telling a story about Mexican-American history and culture. The artwork in Chicano Park is not just beautiful but also deeply meaningful, as it represents the struggles and victories of the people who live there. Many artists still come to the park to create new paintings, making it a living piece of history that continues to grow.

If you love museums and galleries, you'll find plenty to explore in San Diego. The Museum of Contemporary Art in La Jolla is a fantastic place to see modern and experimental art. Some of the pieces in this museum are traditional paintings, while others are interactive exhibits that let you become part of the artwork. The museum also has an outdoor sculpture garden with breathtaking views of the Pacific Ocean, making it a perfect place to enjoy art and nature at the same time. Another great museum is the Timken Museum of Art, which is smaller but filled with masterpieces from famous artists like Rembrandt and Vermeer. Best of all, it's free to visit, making it an excellent stop for young art lovers.

Music festivals are another exciting part of San Diego's creative scene. One of the biggest music festivals in the city is the CRSSD Festival, where electronic and dance music artists perform for huge crowds by the waterfront. The festival has a fun and energetic atmosphere, with people dancing to music under the sun. For those who love jazz, the San Diego Jazz Fest brings together talented musicians from all over the world. The festival takes place every year and features smooth jazz performances that are perfect for relaxing and enjoying good music. If you're a fan of different music styles, the Wonderfront Festival is a must-see event. This festival features rock, pop, hip-hop, and Latin music, and it takes place right by the San Diego Bay, making it a unique experience.

San Diego also celebrates art with special events like ArtWalk, an annual festival that fills the streets with paintings, photography, sculptures, and live performances. It's one of the largest art events on the West Coast, and thousands of artists come to showcase their work. Walking through ArtWalk feels like stepping into an open-air museum where you can talk to artists, watch them create their masterpieces, and even take home a piece of art.

If you enjoy hands-on creativity, there are plenty of places in San Diego where you can make your own art. Studios like the Hot Spot in Point Loma let you paint pottery, while places like Art on 30th offer painting classes for beginners. If you love music, some schools and workshops teach people how to play instruments, write songs, or even record their own music.

San Diego's music and art scenes are full of excitement, talent, and creativity. Whether you're visiting a world-class museum, watching a live band at a cool venue, exploring colorful street murals, or attending a music festival by the ocean, there's always something happening in this artistic city. Creativity is everywhere, from the bustling streets of downtown to the peaceful gardens of Balboa Park. No matter where you go, you'll find artists expressing themselves through paintings, sculptures, performances, and melodies. If you love music and art, San Diego is the perfect place to explore, get inspired, and maybe even create something amazing yourself.

Chapter 20: Sunset Views from La Jolla

San Diego is known for its stunning coastline, and one of the best places to experience a breathtaking sunset is in La Jolla. This seaside neighborhood is famous for its dramatic cliffs, sandy beaches, and sparkling blue waters, making it a perfect spot to watch the sun sink below the horizon. When the sky turns into a masterpiece of colors—shades of pink, orange, red, and purple blending together—it feels like nature is putting on a magical show just for you. Whether you're standing on a cliffside, relaxing on the beach, or exploring a hidden cove, La Jolla offers some of the most unforgettable sunset views in the world. Locals and visitors alike gather every evening to witness this daily wonder, and each sunset is unique, changing with the seasons and the clouds in the sky.

One of the most popular places to watch the sunset in La Jolla is at the famous La Jolla Cove. This small, picturesque beach is surrounded by rugged cliffs that create a natural amphitheater, giving you a front-row seat to the sun's final moments of the day. As the golden light reflects off the ocean waves, sea lions and seals can often be seen lounging on the nearby rocks, adding to the magical atmosphere. Sometimes, pelicans glide across the sky, silhouetted against the glowing backdrop. If you listen closely, you might hear the gentle sound of the waves crashing against the shore, mixing with the distant barking of sea lions. Many people bring blankets and snacks to enjoy a sunset picnic, while photographers set up their cameras, eager to capture the perfect shot of the sun dipping into the Pacific Ocean.

Another incredible spot to catch a La Jolla sunset is at the cliffs of Torrey Pines. This area, home to the famous Torrey Pines State Natural Reserve, offers some of the most spectacular views in San Diego. From high atop the rugged cliffs, you can see for miles out into the ocean, with the sun casting a golden glow over the entire landscape. As you walk along the trails, the fresh scent of pine trees fills the air, mixing with the salty breeze from the sea. The cliffs provide a panoramic view, and when the sun begins to set, the whole sky transforms into a canvas of dazzling colors. On clear days, you can even see all the way to the distant Channel Islands on the horizon. Many hikers time their walks so they can reach a scenic overlook just in time for the sunset, making the experience even more rewarding.

For those who prefer a more relaxing sunset experience, La Jolla Shores Beach is an excellent choice. This long, sandy stretch of beach is perfect for families, surfers, and beachgoers who want to watch the sun set while feeling the cool sand beneath their feet. As the sun slowly sinks lower in the sky, the waves shimmer with golden light, and the water looks like it's glowing. People gather in groups, sitting on towels or beach chairs, chatting and taking photos of the colorful sky. Some even bring bonfires, roasting marshmallows and enjoying the peaceful evening as the sky fades to deep blue. If you're lucky, you might see dolphins playing in the waves, their fins slicing through the glowing water. As the sun disappears completely, the beach lights up with the soft glow of campfires, and the stars begin to twinkle above, marking the end of another perfect San Diego day.

One of the most unique sunset spots in La Jolla is the famous Sunset Cliffs. Although technically just south of La Jolla, this dramatic stretch of coastline is a favorite for sunset watchers. The cliffs rise high above the ocean, providing a stunning view of the waves crashing below. During sunset, the entire area glows with warm colors, and the reflection of the sun on the water creates a dazzling path of light stretching all the way to the horizon. People often sit along the edges of the cliffs, feet dangling over the edge, as they watch the sun make its slow descent. The experience is peaceful yet powerful, with the endless ocean stretching before you and the sound of the waves echoing through the air. Sometimes, if conditions are just right, you can witness a rare phenomenon called the "green flash," a brief green light that appears just as the sun sets. It only lasts for a second, but those who see it never forget it.

Another fantastic place to experience a La Jolla sunset is at Mount Soledad. This hilltop viewpoint is the highest point in the area, offering 360-degree views of San Diego and the Pacific Ocean. When the sun begins to set, the entire city is bathed in warm golden light, and the ocean glows like a sea of fire. As darkness falls, the city lights begin to twinkle, creating a stunning contrast between the natural beauty of the sunset and the man-made beauty of the illuminated city below. The Mount Soledad Veterans Memorial, located at the summit, provides a peaceful setting for reflection and appreciation of the view. Many visitors bring binoculars to spot boats sailing across the glowing water or to catch a glimpse of wildlife moving through the hills.

La Jolla's sunsets are not just about the view—they're also about the experience. Many people love to end their day by taking a sunset walk along the La Jolla Coastal Walk, a scenic path that winds along the cliffs, offering breathtaking ocean views. Along the way, you'll pass hidden coves, tide pools, and rocky outcrops where sea birds nest. The sound of the waves and the fresh ocean breeze make the walk even more enjoyable. As the sun sets, the path is filled with people taking in the beauty of the moment, some holding hands, others quietly reflecting on the day.

For those who enjoy a bit of adventure, kayaking at sunset is an unforgettable experience. La Jolla is known for its sea caves, and guided kayak tours take visitors out onto the water to explore these hidden wonders. Paddling through the gentle waves as the sun sets creates a magical feeling, as the water around you reflects the vibrant sky. Sometimes, bioluminescent plankton light up in the water, making the ocean glow with tiny sparks of light, adding an extra layer of enchantment to the experience.

Dining at one of La Jolla's many oceanfront restaurants is another fantastic way to enjoy a sunset. Restaurants like George's at the Cove,

Duke's La Jolla, and The Marine Room offer stunning views along with delicious meals. Imagine enjoying fresh seafood while watching the sky change colors, the waves rolling in just below your table. Some restaurants, like The Marine Room, are so close to the water that waves actually crash against the windows during high tide, making for an exciting and unforgettable dining experience.

La Jolla's sunsets are a daily reminder of nature's beauty, and whether you watch from a beach, a cliff, a kayak, or a restaurant, the experience is always special. No two sunsets are exactly alike, and each one brings its own unique display of colors and light. Locals and visitors alike never get tired of watching the sun slowly sink into the Pacific Ocean, leaving behind a glowing sky and a peaceful feeling that lingers long after the last rays of light have faded. If you ever visit San Diego, make sure to set aside time to experience a La Jolla sunset—it's one of the most magical moments you'll ever witness.

Epilogue

What an adventure it's been! From the sandy shores of Mission Beach to the historic streets of Old Town, San Diego is truly a place like no other. We've discovered incredible animals at the world-famous San Diego Zoo, soared on thrilling rides at LEGOLAND, and explored the wonders of Balboa Park. Along the way, we tasted delicious Mexican food, heard stories of the past, and watched breathtaking sunsets over the Pacific Ocean.

But even after all these exciting adventures, there's always more to explore in San Diego. This city is full of hidden gems and new experiences just waiting to be found. Who knows? Maybe the next time you visit, you'll discover a new favorite spot or make unforgettable memories with your family and friends.

San Diego is a city of sunshine, smiles, and endless fun. Whether you're building sandcastles on the beach, learning about history, or simply enjoying the vibrant neighborhoods, there's something here for everyone. And no matter where your next adventure takes you, the magic of San Diego will always be waiting for you to return.

So, until next time, keep exploring, keep learning, and keep having fun! Who knows where your curiosity will lead you next?

Farewell for now, San Diego. We'll see you again soon!

The End.